Throw Your Heart Over the Fence

Throw Your Heart Over the Fence

The Continuing Adventure
of the Famous People Players

Diane Dupuy

KEY PORTER BOOKS

This book is dedicated to my husband, Bernard, my two children, Jeanine and Joanne, and to my mother, Mary, who have given me some of my greatest adventures, and helped me believe in angels.

Cataloguing in Publication Data

Dupuy, Diane
    Throw your heart over the fence
ISBN 1-55013-814-6

1. Famous People Players. 2. Puppets and puppet-plays — Canada. 3. Black box theaters.
I. Title.

PN1979.B57D87 1996   791.5'3087'4   C96—931621—6

Key Porter Books Limited
70 The Esplanade
Toronto, Ontario
M5E 1R2

Editor: Philippa Campsie
Line Editor: Mary Adachi

Printed and bound in Canada

96 97 98 99 5 4 3 2 1

Contents

A Few Words About Diane Dupuy

by Don Harron

The first time I met her she was an early morning guest on "Morningside." As the host of that radio show, I was given all kinds of research information about Diane Dupuy and her group, the Famous People Players. I don't remember anything about that interview because "Morningside" is the kind of program where you say good-bye with much effusiveness, and then sweep everything about that person completely out of your mind to clear it for the next interview.

Three weeks later, I was doing a Charlie Farquharson speech at a convention in one of Toronto's big hotels. I forget which one, but I shared the bill with the Famous People Players, and I will never forget the impact they had on me. I had seen black-light theater in the Czech pavilion at Montreal's Expo, but the Diane Dupuy troupe gave it a special glow. After the performance, Diane literally collared me and took me backstage to meet the cast. Dressed as Charlie Farquharson, I was an instant celebrity because all of the Famous People Players were watchers of "Hee Haw" ("Sesame Street" for grown-ups).

Not long after that I got an urgent call from Diane Dupuy asking me to go to the Grand Theater in London, Ontario, and be a substitute narrator for a Famous People Players show based on Saint-Saëns' *Carnival of the Animals*. I replaced the then lieutenant governor of Ontario, Pauline McGibbon, who offered in return to substitute for me sometime. I told Diane to ask Pauline if she could grow a good crop of stubble and wear clothes that would make her look like an unmade bed. Now Diane Dupuy's mother, the marvelous Mary Thornton, has created a Charlie Farquharson puppet who takes over for me on occasions when I can't be there, and makes appropriate gestures and lip syncs to my previously recorded dialogue.

My wife, Catherine McKinnon, has also been deeply involved with Diane and her players. Hardly a day goes by in our lives without a frantic phone call from Dora Doom (Catherine's favorite nickname for Diane). When the Famous People Players made their Broadway debut, Catherine was there as company cheerleader and Diane's personal baby-sitter. Such a need was even greater when the players were greeted with unanimous raves from the New York critics. Diane is, after all, a Canadian, and finds it difficult to cope with international adoration.

Dora Doom immediately focused on the next problem, instead of basking in the latest triumph: "How am I going to find a permanent home for these kids of ours?" That, dear reader, is the story of the book you are about to read. I have already read it, and found it simply written in short, declarative sentences without any jargon, and almost impossible to put down. In fact, I read it at a single sitting.

But Dora's doom continues. Diane Dupuy still lives on a knife-edge trying to provide for her talented brood. Catherine is always on hand, urging her to have faith in the future. "Pray to Saint Anthony, Diane, he's always there for you." Recently, a desperate Diane did just that, and was rewarded with a substantial amount of money from a first-time visitor to the theater home of the Famous People Players.

Our phone rang immediately. "And do you know what, Catherine," said a jubilant Diane Dupuy, "his first name is *Anthony*!"

Prologue

"What? Are you crazy? Who the hell wants another theater, let alone a theater center for the handicapped?" screamed one of the most prominent citizens in our country.

I was shocked. I had called this man hoping to get support for a permanent theater for the Famous People Players, a company of adults who are mentally handicapped and perform with giant puppets using the black-light technique. We call ourselves the Famous People Players because we pay tribute to the music and artistry of famous people, and we are the players.

His response was so negative it was as if a lasso had caught me by surprise, brought me down to the ground, and dragged me into reality.

"How much money is this going to cost?" he demanded.

"Well, I'll need about three million dollars to complete the project."

"*Three million dollars?* Why on earth would you want to attempt this project? This city has too many theaters as it is, why do we need another?"

As he yelled into the phone, I tried to hold back the tears that wanted to erupt from my eyes.

"Are you there?"

I swallowed and said, "We need a theater because our company has been together for fifteen years and I have always been concerned about what would happen to the veterans of the company who no longer perform. Where would they go, and what would become of them? I want to start up a dinner theater with a restaurant, where they will learn how to cook, serve, and further enhance their life skills."

"This is a lot of money," he interrupted. "Let their parents look after them. Why should I give you anything? I get thousands of requests a day from worthwhile organizations and there is only so much money to go around. You have to show me why, out of all the other charities, I should give you money. Start by sending me a proposal." Click, he hung up.

The dial tone rang in my ear and I slumped to the floor, still holding the receiver. The tears poured down. I couldn't control myself. My secretary, Terry Paterson, ran into my office.

"What the hell happened?"

I couldn't stop crying. She thought someone had died. Finally, I stood up, put the receiver back on the phone, and told her what had happened.

"How on earth, Terry, am I ever going to spearhead a capital campaign after this assassination attempt on my dream?" As I wiped the tears from my face, I realized that the one positive thing that had happened was that I'd managed to get one of the busiest men in the country on the phone. The bad news was that he was right: there are thousands of worthy charities, all of them looking for money. The same people are constantly being hit up with thousands of requests. Why should he give anything to the Famous People Players?

I said to myself firmly, "Diane, the Lone Ranger wouldn't take things so personally," and I got back on the saddle to continue my journey. My confidence was badly shaken, but my dream was still intact.

If you ever meet me, you will notice that I have a flat behind from falling on my ass so many times. This book, a sequel to my first book, *Dare To Dream*, is the continuing adventure of the Famous People Players, one dream after another—and, ouch, one fall after another.

1
The Dream

I was born to chase dreams. I knew at a very young age, as I knelt by my bed, praying to my Guardian Angel, that I would never be alone, that my imaginary horse, Silver, would always be by my side as I chased my dreams.

As I grew older and ventured into the outside world, I was amazed by the people I ran into who didn't chase dreams, who had no vision, no imagination, no courage to believe in themselves. They were the losers, I thought, and I often wondered how they had become losers.

When we were kids, we were never ashamed of doing the most ridiculous things, we were never embarrassed or worried about failing. We loved to explore and seek adventure, whether it was playing cowboys and Indians or pretending to be Snow White, waiting for Prince Charming to come along. For us, everything had a happy ending.

When did we lose that naïve courage? Did we lose it because we now live in a world of harsh reality, where not everything has a happy ending?

Teachers in school taught us to use our brains, to think and be smart. They told us that if we weren't smart we would fail, and that failing is a big embarrassment and something to be ashamed of. Winning was everything.

As a child growing up in Hamilton, Ontario, I knew there was more to life than high IQs. But my love of adventure always got me into trouble.

"Stop daydreaming, Diane!" the nuns at school would yell at me. "Concentrate on your work!"

"When I grow up I want to be the Lone Ranger," I would say.

"Nonsense! You dream too much. You are not going to become the Lone Ranger." Slap went the strap on my hand.

As soon as the four o'clock bell rang, announcing the end of school for the day, I became wide awake and full of life. I would run from my desk to my invisible horse, Silver, who waited for me under the tree in the schoolyard. I would pretend to mount him, and with my arms stretched forward as if I was holding onto the reins, I'd gallop home. I'd pick up speed as I started down Hamilton mountain.

Leaping over rocks on the escarpment, beating the traffic as it wound down the mountain road, I knew that the best part of the day was riding Silver home, leaving far behind the classroom that sparked no imagination. Faster and faster I rode, my hair falling out of its pigtails. My heart beat as fast as my horse's hooves. When the bus that I was supposed to take began to catch up to me, I would look back at the driver, who waved at me with a smile.

"He knows," I thought, "he knows my horse can beat him." We would make it to the bus stop just as he opened his doors. Silver had brought me safely to my destination.

Out of breath, I slowly walked to my house, where my mother awaited my arrival.

My mother always recognized my need to dream. She encouraged me to explore my imagination with my puppets. The puppets that she gave me as a child were my first friends. They shared my secrets and never told on me. They understood my need to become the Lone Ranger.

My father, an alcoholic, prepared me for the bumps in life that lay ahead of me. He came to this earth as probably my greatest teacher. When he drank he cut loose with his tongue, which could wound like a knife. The sting of his belt was never as painful as the lash of the words that spewed out of his mouth.

His impatience taught me about patience. His lack of kindness during those drinking periods made me remember to be kind. It was only when he drank or was unhappy that he was like this. His unhappiness wanted me to be happy.

He used to send me to sit in the dark basement for punishment. But I was never afraid of the dark. It was there that I discovered my imagination. I pretended to be Snow White, Sleeping Beauty, even Jiminy Cricket. I acted out all of the Walt Disney movies that Dad took me to see, as my horse, Silver, waited at the top of the staircase for my return.

With my hand puppets, I explored my inner feelings. I would slip them on my hands and whisper, "When you wish upon a star, makes no difference who you are."

When I was six, I was sent to the Sacred Heart School. On my first day a nun slapped me. Was it something I had said? Who knows? I felt I must have deserved it. After all, she was considered one of God's chosen beings.

Each day continued with the taunts and jeers of children in the playground, who called me "Retard." I was afraid to venture outside to play for fear of meeting them. I had never felt such loneliness before. I was alone inside my soul. I prayed over and over again to my Guardian Angel, as Silver waited outside my bedroom window.

When I was told I had to repeat a year of school, I was embarrassed and hurt. I had failed.

One day a new girl came to join the class. She had terrible seizures that made her fall on the floor. When her skirt rode up, revealing her underwear, all the kids would laugh.

"I really don't see what's so funny," I cried.

Things didn't improve much as I got older. As a teenager, I had problems at home, at school, and within myself. Once I was accused of stealing from the till of a department store I worked for. I was sent to the security department and strapped to a lie detector. This would prove my innocence, I thought.

"Well, go ahead, read it," I said when it was over. "And then go ahead and tell Mr. Pinkerton over there that he made a mistake and got the wrong person."

The security officer looked at me in a way that I would never forget. He was at a loss for words, embarrassed, and confused. "It says that you are lying," he said.

I burst out crying. I hadn't taken the money, but no one believed me.

Walking home that night from a job I no longer had, I felt embarrassment and shame. Why was God preventing me from succeeding in life? "I'm not a bad person. Why, why, why?" I kept asking myself. Slowly I began to realize that maybe I was failing because I had joined the rest of the world, hung up my white hat, put away my imagination, and stopped believing in myself.

Tears blinding my vision as I walked, I remembered the wonderful time I used to have riding Silver home from school. Where was he? I missed him. I needed to dream and dream big.

I knew that I had to put on my white hat if I was going to ride away from embarrassment and shame. I realized the answer to my question was waiting for me as I rode into the future.

I have led many lives in this one lifetime. Each part of my life prepared me for what was to come next. I learned from all kinds of people: my father, the nun who slapped me, the children who called me names, the young girl with the seizures, and the store manager who thought I'd stolen money. The lessons were painful, but it was better than not learning at all. Imagine living your entire life with no conflict; no confrontations with others; everything going smoothly, no problems, no challenges. How boring! Along my human journey each day of my life, I have come to understand that the dark angels I come in contact with are important to my spiritual growth. They teach me tolerance of others.

Remembering Einstein's great quote, "Imagination is far greater than knowledge," I founded the Famous People Players with a group of young people who were once called retarded. We felt ashamed and insecure. Believing in our dream, we worked hard to conquer our handicaps and we were able to overcome that awful label. I taught them to perform with life-size puppets using the black-light technique. The stage is lit with ultraviolet light, which reveals only the fluorescent paint on the puppets. The players, who wear black, cannot be seen, so the puppets seem to fly through the air, defying gravity.

When I first started work with the players, I had a superiority complex. I never allowed myself to say things that would have anyone think less of me, or make me ashamed of not having an education. Being boss made me, well, bossy. It's easy to criticize, a lot harder to praise. It's hard to say I'm sorry. It takes strength and courage to say I made a mistake. But I noticed how the players are not afraid to admit they've made a mistake or to say they're sorry. This is something I had great trouble learning, as my pride always got in the way.

But over the years, these young people silently taught me to listen to my soul and to think with my soul. When this happened, I felt a wonderful sense of growth and development. I forgot about myself and became myself. I was slowly finding my life's dream, becoming the Lone Ranger again.

I also learnt from failing, from making an ass of myself, and that's nothing to be ashamed of. In Famous People Players we talk freely about how we can improve ourselves and we cry openly when we find ourselves or members of our family in serious trouble. We are not ashamed to be ourselves. My years with the Famous People Players have changed me to become more like them. I have learned from my mistakes; I never learned a thing from the rave reviews, standing ovations, or awards and rewards we received.

Traveling with the Famous People Players, I saw the world through their eyes. As Forrest Gump said, "Life is like a box of chocolates. You never know what you're going to get." The Famous People Players, for me, do more than just perform magic on stage. They teach me about inner magic, about the human spirit. They show me why we who are born perfectly normal are really abnormal. I'm often amazed that the people who give me the most grief are those who have graduated from the best of schools, have the best education, and come from the best homes. They should know better. The Famous People Players, who do not have these things, know better.

After twenty-three years with the Famous People Players I am continually amazed at how many of us don't use our full potential. We don't share. We don't listen to our inner voices. We waste years of our lives by trying to get even, feeling sorry for ourselves or thinking only of ourselves. We have forgotten to dream. Worst of all, we do not know the meaning of unconditional love. What are we afraid of that we continue to satisfy our needs by ripping people off? When we do that, we shortchange ourselves.

The world has become bottom-line driven. We don't respect other people and we worship technology. In the entertainment industry, the value of what goes on television takes a back seat to money and profits. Sensationalism fills the airwaves, pumping negative thoughts into impressionable youth. Why? Because it increases the ratings, which increases the figures in our bank books.

We teach our children to be angry and violent through popular music. When they hear lyrics like "A bitch is a bitch, is a bitch" or "Don't want no short-dick man" or "Don't want no flat-chested bitch," what are they to think? Our children are the future of the world and in order for them to be free, they have to stop moving, stand still, meditate, and learn that what's inside them is far greater than what's outside.

We invest lots of money on the outside of our bodies—our hair, make-up, clothes—but what price should we pay for our inner selves? Children today do not learn how to reach their inner selves because we, their role models, are too busy following the crowd and thinking of our own survival.

We were all meant to be individuals, to express our individuality. No two snowflakes are ever alike and each snowflake that falls on me brings me to a higher level of understanding of who I am.

When Napoleon was spending his last days in exile, he wrote in his diary that he remembered only five days of happiness in his lifetime. Here was a man who seemingly had everything—power, sex, money, everything. Mother Teresa, who was born into a life of wealth and power, gave up everything for one sari and two pairs of sandals. Yet she says she has never known a day of unhappiness in her life.

What's happened to us? We continue to make ourselves unhappy, lonely, and bitter, even though we have comfortable houses, good jobs, cars, money, and often power. We have to go back to the beginning, when we were children, and get back our imaginations and the dreams we once dreamt.

My dream didn't end with the creation of the Famous People Players —that was just the beginning. Riding on my imaginary horse, Silver, I would lasso one dream and when I caught it, other dreams escaped for me to chase. The dream that kept escaping was the one I wanted so badly. I wanted to create a home, a theater center for the Famous People Players.

When I have a dream, I get a magnificent rush. It's as if I'm a child again riding my horse home from school. I'm flying high. Silver can jump over the tallest trees. There's nothing like having a dream to make you feel high. You're flying, soaring through the air.

I used to get myself into trouble because I was always getting people to follow *my* dream. I kept forgetting that they have their own dreams they should be following. The performers have taught me that Famous People Players is a stepping-stone to other things, "other dreams, Diane."

Now, in the twenty-third year of the Famous People Players, I'm a dream-maker. I dedicate my life to encouraging people to dream, and dream big. My performers say I'm growing up, but there is still much more to learn, lots more before I graduate and go onto another dream.

2
Life with
the Famous
People Players

You can learn a lot from falling on your ass. Being with the Famous People Players day in and day out I learn more about the human spirit, particularly when I fail.

"Diane, it's not that bad," Else Buck once said to me when I was anxious about some problem. She looked up at me with a big smile. "You worry too much," she said with a chuckle, as she tried desperately to remember the combination to her locker. Else always shakes when holding onto something. No one knows why. She is such a pretty girl to look at, you would never think anything was wrong with her, but when you start training her to do the simplest things, she has great difficulty. Yet she carries on, she never gives up.

The human spirit of each of these players picks me up and encourages me to go forward. Their silent ways give me empathy. I have learned about unconditional love from each of them.

Greg Kozak, a small, elfish man who was my first cast member twenty-three years ago, always says "Me forget," when it comes to his parts in the show, but his soul never forgets unconditional love, even when each strenuous rehearsal with me gets worse. He always smiles and understands.

Our brains forget and cannot do the most important thing of all: dream. We dream with our souls. What makes us cry, and cry so deeply, is our souls. The brain doesn't feel, it thinks. The soul doesn't think, it feels.

One of the places I do a lot of dreaming is on the road, as I doze on the bus, or watch the landscape flying by. And I remember, too. Sometimes road trips are so full of memories, it's hard to wake up to the present.

Recently we were on tour, and I was staring out the bus window, remembering a family who had a dream, a dream to join the Famous People Players.

I was introduced to the Billinger boys by a letter that arrived in the mail one morning, more than ten years ago. I opened the letter and out fell a Polaroid picture of a man, heavyset, wearing glasses, standing between what looked like his mother and his father. The letter read:

> The following is a résumé of my son Ted, who is thirty-four years of age. Ted has been at the workshop since he was eighteen. He can't read or write and has a problem with money, but can tell time. Also, he is a little slow to learn, but when he does, it stays with him. He also sings, not as well as his brothers, but sing he does. He is also a very smooth dancer. He is pretty easy to get along with and naturally, he gets put out with his brothers at times.
>
> Maybe, in the future, you may feel that Ted has a place in your future plans.
>
> Yours sincerely,
> Iris Billinger

As I continued to open my mail, I came across another letter. Out fell a picture, which looked exactly like the first one. It was of a young man, heavyset, with glasses, standing between his parents. The letter read:

On behalf of my son Douglas, I'm writing you this letter. Doug is now working in ARC industries, which is a sheltered workshop, and has been since he was eighteen years of age. He is now thirty-four, his birthday is September 25, and he was born in 1950. He is talented in many ways. He can sing and dance very well and is a good worker at home. With Jim Nabors' records he can follow his songs and sings well with him to "Love Me With All of Your Heart," in Spanish.

Doug doesn't know money too well, but thanks to digital watches he can tell time.

He is not happy working in the workshop and I thought maybe he would have talent you could use somewhere.

Sincerely,
Iris Billinger

The third letter, I knew by the handwriting, was once again from Iris Billinger. When I opened it, out fell another photograph. I wondered, looking at the three pictures that now lay spread out across my desk, why she hadn't taken one picture of all three men and sent one letter. It was obvious to me that she wanted them to be treated like individuals. She had a lot of love and respect for Ted, Doug, and Gord.

The third letter was basically the same. It read:

This is the résumé of Gord. On December 1984 he will be thirty years old. He loves music and singing. He plays his radio all night. It helps him to fall asleep. You have seen the pictures of my three sons of whom their father and I are very proud. They are loved.

Respectfully yours,
Iris Billinger

Imagine one set of parents giving birth to three boys who are handicapped. I thought anyone in her right mind would have gone to the doctor to stop having more, but when I met Iris and her husband, Jim Billinger, I soon learned that they knew in their hearts and souls that each child had a purpose. These boys were loved and loved very deeply. They would find their meaning by living life to the fullest, teaching me a very important lesson in unconditional love. That was the beginning of our lives with them.

Shortly after I'd accepted Ted, Gord, and Doug, known as the Billinger boys, into the company, I received a letter from ARC Industries:

> ARC Industries' concern with both these young men is their attendance records. In one year Gord was absent on 119 days and Ted was absent on 123 days. In addition to this, they took sixteen days of holiday. Doug never showed up.

After reading their employment record, I somehow felt in my heart that with a new job challenge at Famous People Players their attendance would improve and their work habits would change. Never did I realize that meeting the Billinger family would change my life.

There was one thing missing from Mrs. Billinger's letters. I would later learn that if you were to look up the word "lazy" in the dictionary, next to it would be the names Ted, Gord, and Doug Billinger. They were the laziest people I had ever met. Doug, who eventually chose not to join the Famous People Players, never showed up for work; he wanted to be a country-and-western star and spent his days singing along with his records and watching his favorite TV program," The Andy Griffith Show." Ted and Gord came in to work, but avoided every chore that was assigned to them. Sometimes we would run around our rehearsal warehouse yelling, "Ted, Gord, where are you?"

"I found them," Benny D'Onofrio would cry out. "They're sound asleep under a pile of props."

"Shame on you," Else would say, wagging her finger at them.

After an exasperating four years with them—it takes a long time to train a challenged person in the black-light technique—we decided to let them go. We were all physically exhausted from trying to motivate those boys, we couldn't find out what made them tick. Taking them on one tour after another only brought the company to tears of frustration as we fought our way through each show.

I have no common sense. The voice in my inner soul insisted they stay. However, I decided to ignore the voice inside me and to use my noodle instead. I would let them go. I would muster up my courage and tell the parents that we were sorry, but there was no way that I could consider keeping them. They were impossible!

I had my big speech all prepared for Mr. and Mrs. Billinger. When they arrived in my cubbyhole of an office, they sat down and I shut the door, getting ready to deliver the axe. "I should have done this years ago," I thought. "Here it is 1988 and four years have passed. I'm such a sucker for people, but enough is enough." I sat down facing them. "I don't care how sweet this couple is," I said to myself, "I can't take their two sons."

"Well, Mr. and Mrs. Billinger," I began. I stared at a pencil on my desk because I didn't have the courage to look them in the eyes. "I called you here to discuss Ted and Gord."

"Oh, Diane, before you start," Iris interjected, "Jim and I have to say something." She held onto her husband's hand. "I know how trying these past four years have been for you and the company, but we wanted you to know that maybe you hadn't seen the improvement in the boys, but we have, and we are so grateful to you and the Famous People Players for what you have done. What a wonderful opportunity you have given us all. If you ever decide to let them go, Jim and I want you to know that we understand and thank you for what you have done for them."

"Today they know the subway system, and how to get around the city. They make their own lunches in the morning, and keep themselves clean," added Jim Billinger.

"Yesterday," Iris said, "Ted brought home the correct change from the grocery store. They have become better people for the wonderful experience you have given them. It's a dream come true for us."

I took a deep breath.

"I called you both here to tell you I'm not giving up on Ted and Gord. I will continue to work with them and keep them for another year. We will not give up."

Shortly after that meeting, Mr. Billinger died, and the Famous People Players and I boarded a bus with two sad and lonely boys to embark on a grueling tour of the United States.

"Everything will be okay," Else said, patting Gord on the back.

"Yeah, we're your family," said Benny.

Highway 90 will never be the same. Each city we went to, things got worse and worse. Ted and Gord did nothing, they didn't even show up for their parts. Their minds were elsewhere.

"We miss our dad," said Ted.

"I know Ted, we all miss your dad, but life goes on," I said.

Years later Else reminded me of her favorite movie, *Rain Man*. In one scene, Tom Cruise gets out of his convertible and chases Dustin Hoffman down the road. "Are you in there, are you listening to me?" he yells.

"It reminds us of you yelling at Ted and Gord," Else told me, laughing.

It wasn't that I gave them anything complicated to do in the show. I gave them two ribbons, long rainbow streamers. All they had to do was wave them in the air. I took their arms, and waved the ribbons with them, and always they would say, "I know Diane, we'll do it." "We promise." "Gotcha." "Don't you worry, dearie, we'll make you proud." "You can count on us."

Right. I could count on them to give me a nervous breakdown. Sitting in the audience, I watched the curtain go up and the ribbons dragging across the floor. Night after night I jumped from my seat in the audience in anger. Some nights I don't know who the audience was watching more, me making a jackass out of myself or the performance by the Famous People Players.

Every night I flew backstage and ranted and raved in the dressing room. I ripped my hair out, jumped up and down in the aisle of the moving bus, screaming at the top of my lungs, trying to get them to hear me, as the bus tore down the highway. "Are you guys in there, are you listening to me?"

One day we arrived at the Paramount Theater in Chicago. As usual, everyone in the company started to set up the stage. As I looked around the empty theater, which was soon to hold three thousand people, I saw Ted and Gord getting ready to preset their ribbons. I grabbed them as they walked by me, and made them face out into the auditorium. As they stood holding their ribbons in their hands, I said, "Look up there!"

They looked up at the third balcony where I was pointing. Then they looked at each other.

"Who's up there?" I asked.

"Nobody," said Ted.

"Look again."

They looked.

"Nobody's there," said Gord.

"LOOK, YOU TWO!" I yelled, stomping my foot. "Your father is up there, and he is looking down at you right now. Now pick up those ribbons and wave to him, and tell him you're going to be all right."

They picked them up and started waving, and when the curtain went up that night those ribbons flew in the air like birds through the clouds. I broke down in a flood of tears and stood up to give them a standing ovation. Considering this was the opening of the show, I must have looked crazy to the rest of audience, but I didn't care.

That evening, after striking the set and loading up the bus, we drove to the next city on the tour. The Billinger brothers led our tired but happy family in songs like "In the Good Old Summertime" and "I Want a Girl Just Like the Girl Who Married Dear Old Dad."

I lay down at the back of the bus, huddled under a blanket, and cried.

"Diane," Benny said shaking my shoulder, "I think they're gonna be all right."

It had taken me all those years to find the right thing to motivate Ted and Gord, who were now so proud of themselves. Seeing their hearts full of love for one another backstage, feeling the emotion that overcame Gord when he took his first bow, watching the pleasure of the other performers as they saw Ted and Gord succeed, I couldn't help crying.

"No more sleeping under the props," said Gord.

I noticed a copy of the *New York Daily Post* on the floor of the bus. The headline read, "I Want The Plaza." Underneath it was a picture of Donald and Ivana Trump, who were going through a divorce. Then it struck me: If Ivana and Donald Trump could sit with me on this bus and experience the moments I experience each day of my life with the Famous People Players, they would indeed be the richest people in the world.

As I curled up in my seat to try to get some sleep, I could hear in the distance Ted and Gord leading the Famous People Players in singing the "Green, Green Grass of Home."

"Ivana, you can have the Plaza," I thought, "I want the bus."

Life isn't about owning and possessing buildings or material things. It's about human beings coming together and sharing, loving, caring, helping—giving, rather than taking. When you do all these things, you end up possessing a wealth of wonderful gifts that make you rich in spirit.

You can feel the way that Mother Teresa feels every day when she extends herself beyond what she thought she could do. Or you can end up like Napoleon, with power and material possessions, but never having known happiness. Don't get me wrong. I love staying at five-star hotels, being pampered and spoiled, and having nice clothes. I also know, for me, that when I'm in that situation for too long, I don't appreciate what I have. I know, whether I like it or not, that I have always functioned and appreciated the finer things in life when I'm staying at motel hell. I try harder, I dream more. Having or living with nice things makes us feel comfortable. Going out on a limb and helping somebody else makes us feel fulfilled.

❋

I sat staring out of the bus window and thinking about the Billingers. Debbie Lim broke into my thoughts. "We are being interviewed on television tonight," she reminded me. "The Curly Show."

Debbie is a tiny Filipino girl who has been with the company for sixteen years. Her mother had rubella when she was pregnant and Debbie was born with serious eye problems. Today she is practically blind. She spent her childhood and adolescence in a school for the handicapped. But when Debbie performs, there is no flaw or anything abnormal about her. She creates beauty on stage with feeling and love. Sitting in the audience, you applaud with your heart as she flies through the air with confidence and peace. She makes her characters and props take on a life of their own. She gives them a soul from her soul.

Outside the security of the stage, Debbie has trouble walking. She bumps into things because she can't see where she is walking. She reminds me of Mr. Magoo, the wonderful cartoon character created by the late Jim Backus. Debbie, like Mr. Magoo, never gets hurt or falls down a manhole. She runs errands all over the city, doing the banking or delivering parcels to corporate offices. She does all this with a smile, and with love and patience for the people she comes in contact with. Whenever I get down in the dumps, I lean on Debbie for strength. Somehow she magically helps me find the answer.

When I thought about "The Curly Show," I felt gloomy. First, we had a performance in Montreal the next day and doing "The Curly Show" meant we had to delay the tour bus for four hours before we could leave. This would mean we'd get no rest before the show. Second, we just didn't feel comfortable about it. It wasn't that we didn't like talk shows. We'd been the subject of numerous American talk shows, such as "The Phil Donahue Show," "Good Morning America," and "Regis and Kathie Lee," and we'd spent a week with Steve Kroft, who is now a correspondent for "60 Minutes." But the producers of "The Curly Show" didn't seem to understand our mission. However, it made sense to do this show because of the national exposure.

Three of us arrived backstage at "The Curly Show" with knots in our stomachs. Curly would be interviewing two of my performers, Benny D'Onofrio and Debbie Lim, as well as me.

Curly entered the dressing room. "Hi and welcome. Now, I want to tell you about MY show and how MY show will run. We have on the show today two guests who are involved in athletics and sports. They are disabled. There's another guest, a blind comedian, and you, the Famous People Players. Now each of you will tell your stories and at the end, a psychologist will come and make her assessment comments about——"

This immediately set off warning bells.

"I hope she's not going to analyze us just because we are handicapped," I said quickly. "Famous People Players deserve respect. We are professional artists. We were not treated like this on 'The Phil Donahue Show.'"

Curly stomped her foot. "This is MY show. You don't tell me who to have on MY show. The show runs MY way, not your way." Her face was getting red. "When you are on MY show, you will do as I say."

"Look, Curly," I said calmly, "I was only making a valid comment."

"Well," she responded, "maybe it was your tone of voice. Just remember this is MY show. Now does anyone have any questions to ask me about MY show?"

Debbie Lim smiled, put her hand up, and said, "Yes, I do. What's the name of your show?"

I smiled, thinking about Debbie's question to Curly. I looked around the bus at the players who were playing cards, knitting, sleeping. I noticed two of our staff members talking quietly together. I thought about some of the staff members we'd had over the years. Some truly dedicated people have worked with us, people who have continued the relationships that they developed with the players long after they've left the company.

A couple of staff people who were very special to all of us at Famous People Players were Tom O'Donald and Kamile Smith. They were kind-hearted people who always helped out whenever they could. Once they met a women called Geraldine who had been in an accident, which had left her blind. They asked me if it would be all right to have Geraldine come in one or two days a week to work in our office. They planned to teach her how to do office work.

"It's important for us to get Geraldine back into society again, get her working with other people," Tom explained.

"We'll work with her on our own time," said Kamile with enthusiasm.

I was really impressed at their willingness to help this woman. Geraldine was thrilled. "Just call me a volunteer," she said, beaming.

With the help of Tom and Kamile, Geraldine gained confidence. After spending two months with Famous People Players, she was trained for office work, and before she left she sold an ad in our theater program. Everyone was so happy when Terry, Kamile, and Tom presented her with a commission check. I wondered where Geraldine was now, and how she was doing.

The bus arrived at the theater and we unloaded our things. I walked out onto the stage, the empty stage, which in three hours would suddenly transform itself into a black-light aquarium, filled with fluorescent fish of all shapes and sizes. I could almost hear the audience oohing and aahing, as their eyes caught a glimpse of a mermaid coming out of a sinking ship with a skin diver following close behind.

I watched Benny carrying props into the wings and suddenly remembered an incident a few years ago. We'd just finished a very successful run on Broadway and were touring the United States. It was a typical arrival. Ted was out in the loading dock directing the truck as it started to back up to the loading door.

"Keep going some more," he said, his arm directing the truck to back up. "Keep going...."

CRASH!

The truck slammed into a concrete wall.

"You can stop now," said Ted.

"It's okay," said Else, "there's no damage to the wall."

Everyone unloaded and set up the stage. Debbie Lim was bumping into boxes as she searched for her props by feeling around with her hands.

Gord made a mad dash to me.

"Diane, the Mamas and the Papas are getting back together."

"No, Gord," I replied. "I don't think so."

"Yes, they are," he insisted. "Ed Sullivan said so last night on TV."

Gord was helping set up the stage, lifting Michael Jackson, the singing idol of the 1980s, from his prop box. The puppet's legs folded up around his neck. I'm sure if the real superstar could see this, he wouldn't approve of the fourth-rate accommodations at the Famous People Players.

Performers were carrying props and puppets with pride to their designated spots in the wings. Soon the Famous People Players would turn the stage into one electrifying show. Michael would moonwalk across the stage, leaping across two half-moons, Ted and Gord's new parts.

"Diane," said a man tapping me on the shoulder. I turned around to face a tall, slim man with a neat moustache.

"I want to introduce myself. I'm the general manager and I'd like to welcome you and Famous People Players to our theater. All of us here are really excited. We've heard so many wonderful things about the troupe. The stage looks great. I can't wait to see the show, but I have a small problem I thought I should share with you." He moved aside so we could speak privately. "It's one of your performers, a short, round boy with a moustache."

Benny, I thought. I wasn't looking forward to hearing what he had to say.

"While the group was setting up the stage, he went out to the concession stand in the front lobby and took a box of chocolate bars. I saw him carry it into the men's room where he stayed for almost an hour."

I wondered why I hadn't noticed him missing.

"After he left, I went into the men's room and there was the empty box and chocolate bar wrappers all over the floor. Forty-two of them," he said, laughing. "Can you believe he actually ate all forty-two chocolate bars?"

I really didn't see the humor in it. I was furious.

"Well, he will have to apologize and pay you for the chocolate bars," I told the manager.

"No, no, I wasn't thinking of anything like that," he replied.

"Why?" I asked. "Because he's handicapped? He has to learn just like anybody else. If he was a member of your staff he'd be in serious trouble if he stole a box of chocolate bars, right?"

I waited while he thought about this.

"No, after tonight's performance I want you to go to Benny and tell him you either want the money for the box of chocolate bars or the chocolate bars themselves."

Without giving him any opportunity to reply, I made the decision for him. He seemed a bit surprised by my methods, but he agreed.

As I watched the performers that evening, I kept thinking of Benny and wondering why he had taken the chocolate bars in the first place, let alone eaten all forty-two. I couldn't believe it.

The show was magnificent. Tap shoes magically shuffled across the stage to the music of "42nd Street." On came Streisand's tugboat from *Funny Girl*, pulled by Benny. As it passed the Statue of Liberty, the audience went wild. Watching Benny perform, I wondered how he could move that boat in the dark so smoothly after gorging on forty-two chocolates bars.

The final number amazed me even more. In the "Give My Regards to Broadway" number, Benny played a New York cop directing traffic as two yellow cabs went by. He was amazing. His energy was high voltage as he chased a mugger who steals a purse from a New York Guardian Angel.

As the curtain came down, the company bowed to a standing ovation. Benny, with an enormous smile on his face, was enthralled with the response. No, I thought, he couldn't have done it, he wouldn't have. There must be some mistake. But the general manager had been so sure of what he'd seen.

Quickly, I made my way through the crowd backstage to the dressing room. Everyone was excited.

"Good show, good show," the stagehands said, patting the players on the back.

The cast members were hugging each other.

"Everyone loves us," said an elated Ted and Gord.

"You were good tonight," said Debbie Lim to Benny, "but next time, don't blow that police whistle so loud in my ear. I have enough problems with my eyes, I don't want to lose my hearing too."

"Everyone, pack up, it's time to strike the stage and move on." The stage manager's voice boomed over the dressing-room speaker.

The room was emptying when the general manager walked in.

"Oh, except for you." He took Benny aside and shut the door. "I saw you when everyone was setting up the stage this afternoon. You went into my concession stand and stole a box of chocolate bars. Then you locked yourself in the men's washroom and ate all forty-two of them."

Benny's face was calm. "I what?" he said. "I never did that, Diane." He looked at me. "Why would I do that? And how could I eat forty-two chocolate bars? Wouldn't I be sick?"

The general manager was puzzled. "I saw you," he repeated. His voice changed from an understanding tone to a tone of annoyance. "Look, don't lie to me. I saw you. I want my money back and I want it now."

Once again Benny turned to me for support. "Diane, you gotta believe me. I would never hurt the company this way. This man is lying."

That did it. The general manager was suddenly very angry.

"You know something, Benny," he said. "I saw a show tonight, a beautiful wonderful show, a show I haven't seen in a long time in theater. A show of great magic, sincerity, and love from some very special people who worked like a team so that everyone in the audience went home happy. They did, all of them. Now, how are they going to feel when tomorrow they read next to your rave review that

Benny, one of the Famous People Players, was arrested by the police for stealing from my theater?"

Benny was silent.

The general manager looked at me. "I'm sorry. I'm going to have to call the police."

Frozen with fear, I stared at Benny. Me and my bright ideas, I thought. Through my tears I saw the manager turn toward the phone and lift the receiver.

The silence broke.

"I did it," said Benny. "Just like you said. I did it." He started to cry. "I didn't mean to, honest I didn't."

I was crushed.

"How much do I owe you?" he said. "I'll pay it from my per diem."

I was paralyzed. Benny had not only stolen, he had lied.

Benny paid the manager, counting the money out with his hands shaking, and left quickly to help load the truck. He was glad to get out of the dressing room.

The performers could tell something was wrong when they noticed him wiping the tears from his eyes to lift the box holding the Liza Minelli puppet onto the truck.

"Well, you certainly taught me something," the general manager said to me. "You have to treat them just like anybody else. You know, I wasn't really going to call the police. I just wanted to scare him a little."

"Thank you," I said. "I believe he has learned a big lesson."

That night, after the company had finished loading the truck, all the cast members gathered in the dressing room. Their inner voices had told them something was wrong. Some sat on tables, others turned chairs around and straddled the seat, propping their chins on the backs.

"I did something real bad," Benny said, as he sat facing the group. I could see his reflection in the mirrors, which reminded me of the time he first joined the company nineteen years ago. His first performance had been a bomb. He'd sat in the dressing room crying his heart out, and I'd seen dozens of little Bennies in one mirror after another.

"When you were all working hard setting up the stage, I snuck off and went to the lobby of the theater and stole a box of chocolate bars from the concession stand. I went into the washroom and ate them." He gulped. "I'm so sorry I hurt the company," he sobbed.

Immediately everyone got up and hugged each other and started to cry. Benny was still sitting there, very much alone.

"I tell you why I did it." Everyone sat down again. "I want a girl-friend so much and nobody wants to be my girlfriend because," he started pounding his head with his fists, "because there is something wrong with me!"

I spoke up quickly.

"Lots of people have no girlfriends."

"Oh yeah? Well, you explain this. I asked Bernadette out for coffee three times," he said pointing at one of my staff assistants. "She said no. She said," he stretched his arm out toward her, "she said, 'Benny we work together. We can't go out together.'" He reached for the box of Kleenex on the shelf above him and blew his nose. "Then what did she do? She went for coffee with John." He pointed at another one of my staff assistants, waving his arms in the air. "When I put my arm around her, she doesn't like it, but when John puts his arm around her, she doesn't tell him to stop."

I wanted to say more to Benny, but he interrupted.

"No, not now. I want to be left alone. I just wanted to tell you all why I did it. I was mad and I'm sorry."

At Famous People Players, our handicapped performers work alongside the non-handicapped staff people. They are role models, but in fact all the cast members learn a lot from each other. There are times, however, when I find that some people are insensitive to problems like Benny's.

Looking for staff performers is always a challenge. We need people who are strong and athletic enough to do cartwheels and handstands, and who have a sense of humor. This means eighteen- to twenty-five-year-olds, with the strong bodies of dancers. When they first join the company they often love to be boss, to show they're smarter and know more, but in fact they still have a lot to learn. They have to learn about respect and dignity, compassion and empathy. Some leave the company angry because it's not for them. Others stay and learn and develop true friendships with the players. When this happens you see people forgetting about themselves, becoming themselves.

But now I didn't know what to say. It was hard for me to watch Benny like this. He is a strong young man who had allowed himself to expose his inner self, his vulnerability, to show his true feelings.

The snow was falling heavily that night. Everyone boarded the bus. It was quiet, only the motor of the bus could be heard. As the wheels turned faster and faster, they seemed to say, "We love Benny, we love Benny." Shortly before midnight, Benny threw up the forty-two chocolate bars.

3

The Search Begins

No matter how taxing on the nerves it may be to get Ted, Gord, Benny, Else, and Debbie Lim to learn the simplest things, they have shown me that they are masters of the human spirit. For me, the effort is always rewarding, and I'm grateful to the Famous People Players for letting me be a part of their world. Through their performances, they show us the light. It's funny how we all sometimes choose the dark.

They inspired me not to give up on my dream to create a home for the Famous People Players and the first theater center in the world for people with special needs, no matter how many times I failed in the process. I had to remind myself that if I failed, it was for a reason. I had to assess myself and my direction, learn from my failures, go forward with the knowledge gained from past experiences, and use that experience to succeed.

I knew that finding a home wasn't going to be easy. It would be like mounting a new production, but on a much bigger scale. We needed a producer, someone to help with the money so we could have a stage, sets, props, lights, and "ACTION," as Benny put it. It turned out to be even harder than I thought it would be. Believe me when

I say that I felt that the players and I were on a roller-coaster ride, going up and down, round and round. "I want to get off," I said at times. "Give me a break!" But no. Up and down, then backward again, and round and round I went, backward and forward, then backward again. It never stopped.

In 1984 I thought I'd found a producer. After much cajoling and many meetings at his office in Washington, I actually got John Henry, one of the powerbrokers of Wall Street, to visit the Famous People Players workshop in Toronto. At the time we were working out of a warehouse on Lansdowne Avenue in the west end of the city. He had agreed to help me fundraise and get the dollars needed to make our dream a reality. Better yet, he was going to bring an influential Canadian businessman, Michael Big, who had already endeared himself to people who are handicapped. There was hope. We were going to make it, after all.

Everyone was excited. We prepared for their visit at one o'clock carefully. We waited and we waited for them to show up. One o'clock came and went. One-thirty. Nothing. Two o'clock, still no sign. Two-thirty. When the phone rang, it was John Henry wanting to know if his friend had arrived.

"Not yet," I said.

I don't know how many phone calls he made to me that afternoon, as the performers waited to do a little show for them. He finally called at three o'clock to find out if I had heard anything. I hadn't. When I asked him where he was, he replied that he was outside my front door, calling from his car phone. He had been there all afternoon, but out of respect for his friend he hadn't wanted to come in until the friend arrived.

I went to the front door, and there he was, in his stretch limo, wheeling and dealing on his car phone. It was raining hard, so I took an umbrella and went up to the car door. He looked at me through the window and continued what seemed to be a very serious conversation on the phone.

I stood there in the pouring rain looking at him and thinking to myself, "You need his help. He can raise money just by making a few phone calls from his car phone."

After a long time, the electric window rolled down. I asked him to come in and wait, but he insisted he'd rather wait in his car because he had a lot of phone calls to make. After all, time is money.

Unfortunately for us, Michael Big had completely forgotten the appointment. He called to apologize to all of us for letting us down. "Maybe next time," he said.

Finally, I convinced the American businessman at least to come in and say hello to the performers, who were most anxious to see him and show him their facilities. We showed him around the warehouse. "Here's where we rehearse. Here's the prop room." I was very nervous, trying to please him with the tour.

Each player came forward to shake his hand.

"Hi, my name is Ted. This is my brother Gord."

"I'm Else."

"Hello, I'm Darlene." Darlene Arsenault smiled at him.

"Good afternoon, I'm Debbie Rossen." She curtsied.

"We call her Rossen," said Benny as he introduced himself.

"I'm Lisa." Lisa Tuckwell's mouth opened wide, showing more gums than teeth. She placed Debbie Lim's hand in his hand.

"I'm Debbie Lim. It's nice to meet you. Thank you for coming. We're going to do a little show for you."

"No," he replied. "I honestly don't have any time. I've waited long enough. Perhaps another time, when my friend and I are together."

I thought to myself, not everyone understands or believes in every cause, but at least I was able to get one of the busiest men on Wall Street to visit the Famous People Players. It was a good first step. The second step was to win him over and make him fall in love with our dream.

"That's one busy man," said Else. "He's always on the phone."

"Don't worry, Diane, he'll come and see us perform," said Lisa.

"Yeah, when we open the building," said Gord.

❈

We were in rehearsal one day, trying desperately to get Else to hold her seaweed in the Aquarium number without shaking too hard. My secretary, Terry Paterson, ran in to tell me that John Henry was on the phone.

"See, I told you," Else said. "Don't give up, Diane. You worry too much."

I nervously picked up the receiver.

"Oh, Diane, sorry it's taken so long to get back to you. I'll make it brief. Michael Big, the friend I was telling you about, is very well connected with a development company called, believe it or not, the Famous Players Development Corporation. They would like to build your building at no cost to you and your group. The deal is simple. The city has property downtown. The developers want to build condominiums and the sales from the condos will help pay for the Famous People Players theater, which will be on the ground floor of the building. I want you to go to the city and meet with the property department and see what both our needs are."

I was ecstatic. No, I was more like a rocket that someone had ignited. BANG! I shot up into space. "Guess what?!" I screamed out for everyone to hear. I felt I was riding my horse, Silver, again as the words tumbled out faster and faster. Everyone was trying to follow what I was saying.

"I told you not to worry," said Else, pointing her finger at me.

"We got a home," said Gord.

"Can I call my mother and tell her?" asked Ted.

"Tell the world," I said. "We have a home."

Sleeping the next few nights was difficult. I was full of excitement, waiting for my big meeting with the planners at the city of Toronto.

"Diane, stop kicking. You've got all the blankets and I'm cold," my husband, Bernard, complained, half in French and half in English. The French part was the swear words.

Finally, there I was at City Hall in Toronto. The developer from Famous Players Development Corporation outlined his plans. The building would be designed with extra floors on top that would house condominiums. It was in the heart of Toronto on King Street East. "Sales from the condos will pay for the Famous People Players theater center, at no cost to the Famous People Players," he said to the planners. "We'll need approval from the historical board, however, as the building that is there now is considered a heritage building," he added.

At first everything went smoothly. The designs for our theater center and restaurant were gorgeous.

"Look," said Benny, "I will be the doorman and stand right there."

"That's so you can watch all the girls go by," said Else.

The mayor of Toronto, Art Eggleton, a great supporter of the Famous People Players, did everything to help us get our project up and running. But there were dozens of bureaucratic hurdles. We had to get so many people's approval.

The façade of the building had to be torn down to allow for the extra footage we needed. This was a particularly sore point for some of the bureaucrats. Meeting after meeting in the mayor's office didn't seem to make people from the other departments bend, particularly the representatives of the historical board.

It was then that I had the good fortune to meet a wonderful man and lobbyist, Ivan Fleischmann. He had been brought in by the development corporation to help move the project along. Ivan, a good-looking lawyer/businessman, was cool and calm as he met with each politician and patiently explained over and over again what we wanted to do.

"This is a difficult problem," Ivan said, sitting in the mayor's office. "People get very emotional about historical buildings. The historical board is understandably anxious to preserve old buildings, but that doesn't mean we can't win them over to our side."

"You, Dupuy," (he always calls me that) "are going to come with me and tell your story as only you can tell it to the commissioner of planning. We have to get him on our side."

I met the commissioner for lunch at a restaurant near where we wanted to build our theater.

"We need a home," I told him. "We're lucky that this developer is willing to build a home for Famous People Players for free. If this falls through, where are we ever going to find someone to pay to help us build our theater center? Please help us bring the historical board around to our point of view."

The commissioner was thrilled at the prospect of the Famous People Players making their home at the King Street site. "I'll do the best I can," he promised. "I believe in your dream."

"I've won him over," I thought.

After the lunch meeting, Ivan said to me, "It's not over yet, we're just beginning. You, Dupuy, have to go to each councillor and sell each one on your dream."

"Every single councillor?" I asked.

"No, just the ones that have influence over the others. The ones who can sway the vote," he replied.

Every day after that it seemed that Ivan dragged me off to meeting after meeting at City Hall. I hated lobbying, and it amazed me to think that Ivan did this for a living.

Some councillors had no imagination when I tried to describe what the theater would mean for Toronto. "We have the CN Tower and soon we will have the SkyDome," I'd tell them. "We're the greatest city in the world!"

"So, do you want to run for mayor?" one of them asked me.

Ivan liked this idea. "That's the next step, Dupuy. After we get you your home, you can run for mayor."

"Mayor! Why would I ever want to be a mayor?"

"We need a woman, a strong one. Why not you?"

I sank down in my chair in Ivan's office. "Don't be ridiculous. Count me out. I'm not interested in dealing with politicians every day of my life."

For the next year, we worked hard with the architects to redesign the building to meet everyone's needs. In between the design sessions, Ivan and I ran from one councillor to another. More meetings in the mayor's office. More meetings with the historical board.

"Help us, please help us," I pleaded. "We need the extra space, we have to change the façade. We need to restructure the building. You have to allow us to take down the façade."

"It doesn't matter what you want to do with it," replied the representative from the historical board. "If need be, I will lie down in front of the bulldozer that tries to destroy that façade."

"But it's made out of cardboard. It's falling apart on its own," I kept insisting. "How can we work our way around this?" I looked to the representative from Famous Players Development Corporation for support.

"We need every square foot in order to succeed with the design of the building," he told the representative.

The battle went on for almost six months. Even Mayor Eggleton was having difficulty persuading the planning department, historical board, and the commissioners to bend a little. Fighting City Hall was like riding the roller-coaster backward. Everyone seemed to be walking backward instead of forward. I guess that's because they couldn't see what was in front of them. In the end, the project was cancelled, and we lost a developer who was willing to absorb all the costs of building our home. We were heartbroken.

We had to start all over again. Mayor Eggleton kept trying to help us find a new location. But whenever we thought we were getting close, someone came along and snatched the building from under our noses.

Ivan and I spent a week with a member of the planning department, looking at numerous empty warehouses. One was perfect, but it had no loading dock for the backstage entrance and there was no room on the property to build one. In another the ceiling was too low, or there were too many pillars. Some would have been too expensive to renovate, some were in remote locations that were too hard to get to.

Just as we were about to give up from exhaustion, we found the perfect place. It was a grand old two-story building on King Street

West that looked and felt like home. It had huge windows, hardwood floors, and a spectacular view of downtown Toronto and the CN Tower. It was for sale for $950,000. It was way out of our league, but we thought we would try to see if the owner would let it go for less.

"Yeah, like for nothing," said Benny.

All the parents and the players got together for a tour of the site.

"I love the light coming in the windows," Ron Secker, our volunteer sound engineer, commented.

"The floors are gorgeous," said Mary Thornton, my mother and the head of our prop department. "But how are we going to keep them clean? One scratch from the performing boxes will ruin them."

Totally ignoring my mother, I continued to show off the building. "We can put the prop shop here," I said. "We'll rehearse over there, and the restaurant will be just as you walk in."

"We have a big parking lot out the back," said Benny. "Enough to hold a hundred cars."

I watched Benny try to count all the potential cars that would park on the lot.

"Where are we going to get the money?" asked Else.

"Don't worry," I said.

"What about the taxes?" my mother asked.

"I believe the mayor is going to waive them for us," said Judi Schwartz, our secretary-treasurer.

Everyone agreed it was worth the wait. The architects Brisbin, Brook, Beynon had come that morning and said it was a good building for us. They were putting together a budget for a small theater and restaurant.

"Wherever are we going to get the money?" Ron said in a worried voice. "We were counting on having a developer construct the theater for us for free. Now we're looking at buying a piece of property. How are we going to manage?"

"I'm not worried," I said. "The down payment will come from the money that I have earned traveling all over the United States doing speaking engagements."

"Diane," my mother piped up, "are you out of your mind? You have a family and two children. May I remind you that Jeanine and Joanne need their education to be paid for."

"As far as I'm concerned, I'm not here to win awards, or receive recognition," I replied. "I'm here to make a contribution, to make a difference. This dream is important to me and my family, who have become better people for knowing the Famous People Players."

The next morning, Mayor Eggleton sent a beautiful letter of support to accompany our offer to the owner of the building.

"I can't wait, I just can't wait," said Debbie Lim. "I'm dying to get out of here. It's so dark and gloomy in the warehouse where we are now."

"You're really happy, aren't you, Diane?" Rossen leaned over to me. Looking me straight in the eye, she pressed her forehead to mine. Debbie Rossen has trouble looking after herself, but she excels in looking after me.

"Yes, Rossen, I'm very happy."

Why wouldn't the phone ring? We all started to pace. Nobody could concentrate on rehearsals. Finally, after forty-eight hours the phone rang. It was Judi Schwartz.

"It's a no-go. They want their asking price."

"We don't have the money," I shrieked. "Let me go see the owner. I'll plead our case."

All of us walked over to our dream home and knocked on the office door. The door opened.

"We're looking for the owner of this building," I said.

"I'm the owner."

We were all taken aback. He couldn't have been more than twenty-five, an attractive Japanese man. He graciously welcomed us into his office.

"We're the Famous People Players."

"I know who you are," he said, smiling. "I've seen you on television many times. I love what you do."

He started to shake hands with each of the performers.

"And you're Diane," he said as he came toward me.

"If you love what we do, then you'll let us have this building!" I pleaded with him. "You've got to help us."

"Your reputation precedes you. I'm not surprised you came over here unannounced," he replied. "I want you to know," he said as he started to walk around his office, "this building is a great investment. It's worth a lot more than the asking price. Follow me."

He took us out to the back of the building, to the empty parking lot.

"Look at this land. It's worth the price of two buildings. I could build another building here and lease it out for space. This is a seller's market and I'm doing you a favor by selling it in the first place for the price of $950,000. But my price is firm, I will not let it go for one dollar under the asking price. You must know someone who will give you a donation or a grant."

"We don't receive grants," I said.

"You have lots of friends in high places. The mayor wrote me a letter of support for your offer. That was impressive."

"But not impressive enough," I said.

"Well, Diane, when it comes to money, no. Not impressive enough."

We slowly walked back to our dark, old warehouse.

"He was nice, Diane," said Benny.

"Yeah, but not nice enough," I said.

We tried everything we could think of to raise the extra money. The banks turned us down for a mortgage, as we had no assets. A month later, the building sold for the asking price. Within a short period of time the new owner sold for $2 million. I was heartsick.

It took almost another three years before any luck came our way. This was largely because most of the buildings available were way out of our league financially, and because dealing with City Hall was so frustrating. Elections brought changes, new councillors, and this meant starting all over again. Talking to councillors one by one, selling them on my dream, starting at square one. "Hello, my name is Diane Dupuy and I'm with the Famous People Players..." over and over again.

Thankfully Art Eggleton was still mayor. He asked the new planning commissioner and the people in the planning department to keep trying to help us find a home.

One day in 1987 we got a call. "Great property on Eastern Avenue up for sale," said one of the planners.

We drove there immediately. It was a magnificent building, strong and tall, just like the Famous People Players. I could even see the neon sign over the entrance: "The Famous People Players." When the doors opened I almost had a heart attack from happiness. It was like an airplane hangar, 20,000 square feet of free space without pillars, and the view at the end of the room was a miracle. We could once again see the CN Tower in the distance. I started to cry for joy.

"Quick, call Judi Schwartz, get the architects on the phone, call all the board members and the parents." I was waving my arms with excitement. I could hear the Lone Ranger theme song playing in my head. I jumped and danced all around the huge room. "It's more space than we need," I thought, "but we'll grow into it."

The board, architects, and the parents arrived. Everyone loved the building. Judi ran back to the office of Pat Anderson, our lawyer, to start executing the deal. We couldn't wait for the papers to be drawn up, as the players and I had to get on a flight the next morning to open at Sea World in Orlando, Florida.

By the time we arrived in sunny Florida, a fax was waiting. "Need your signature on the offer. Will deliver it to you tomorrow. Everything looks good, keep your fingers crossed. Love, Judi."

We moved into the Seaworld theater, our home for the next seven months. Everyone was excited as they set up their stage.

"I'll enter from this wing," said Debbie Lim to Benny. "So don't use this entrance, or you'll knock me down."

"Did everyone hear that?" I called out. "Debbie will be using this wing, everyone else use the other one."

"When you finish with your seaweed, pick it up and run toward stage left, then you go to your oyster shell," Michelle Busby said to Lesley Brown. "That way, you will get to your part and you won't miss your cue."

As I stood at the back of the theater, watching Janet, our stage manager, wiring the sound equipment, I heard a huge fight break out on stage. Janet and I ran up to the stage to see Debbie Rossen and Else in a fight.

"I did not."

"Oh, yes, you did," said Else.

Rossen's hair was hanging down in front of her eyes, hiding her tears. Her face was redder than her hair.

"Diane, she hit me because I was talking to Benny," said Else.

"I did not."

"Oh, yes, you did," repeated Else.

"It's true," said Benny. "Rossen hit her. She gets jealous when I talk to the girls all the time."

"I didn't mean to," Rossen said crying. I grabbed her by the shoulders. "I'm sorry," she said quickly. "I have no mother, no father," she cried. Her eyes were puffy and her head and shoulders were bent over. She looked at Benny. "You always talk to Else, what about me?"

"Benny," I said, "remember the chocolate bars and how mad you were at Bernadette and John?"

"Yeah," he said nodding his head.

"You're doing the same thing to Rossen they did to you."

"I'm sorry, Diane. I'm sorry, Rossen," he said.

"Now look, guys, we're not babies, are we?"

"No," Rossen said.

"We're adults, right?" I looked straight at Rossen.

"Yes," she said.

"We're professionals and we don't go around hitting people when we get angry. Now we have a show to do, RIGHT?"

"RIGHT," said Rossen.

"Then let's get on with it," I said.

They started to walk away and I could hear Rossen talking under her breath.

"Rossen, Else," Janet said, "give each other a hug."

They turned and hugged each other.

"Sorry," said Else, "I'll help you from now on. I'll be your sister."

"Okay," said Rossen with a smile and they went back to work.

Janet looked at her watch, "Damn, I'm behind schedule getting the stage set up." She leapt off the stage and took long strides back to the sound booth.

Opening night was festive, and the ice sculptures of Shamoo the Whale made us all feel we had reached the pot of gold at the end of the rainbow.

The next day we read our reviews, which were all glowing. But the most important thing I wanted to read was the offer to purchase that awaited my signature. When the papers came, I proudly autographed them and sealed the envelope with a kiss before sending it back to Pat.

The next two days, I was as nervous as a cat, waiting for the phone or the fax machine to ring. I left the door open to my apartment so I could join the players around the pool and still hear the phone ring.

"We have to do fifty laps in the pool," Rossen said. "Ted says he doesn't have to."

"Yeah, he told me to take a hike," added Debbie Lim.

"He's in his apartment watching TV and he won't come out," said Lesley, giggling.

I went over to his door and banged on it so loud that every apartment door opened to see what was happening. Ted peeked out at me from behind the drapes.

"Surprise! It's me. Open the door, Ted." I pressed my face up to the window, creating a breathmark on the pane.

Ted opened the door. "Ah, Diane, I was just getting my bathing suit on to go for a swim."

"Great, Ted, glad to hear that. Now, hurry up."

"Right away, Diane. I'm coming as fast as I can." Splash! he went into the pool.

"Ted, you don't mind if I have the company count as you swim, do you? You need to do fifty laps."

Ted looked as though he was going to drown right then and there.

"I'll stay here and help you, Ted," said Else.

"Diane, telephone!" Rossen yelled. We all ran toward my apartment. "It's Ron Secker calling from Toronto." She waved the receiver in the air.

"Judi just called me," Ron told me. "We've got the property! The owners were ecstatic it was for the Famous People Players."

"Finally, after all this time, we've got ourselves a home," I said. "What a relief." I collapsed on the couch. "Here." I passed the phone back to Rossen. "Ron has something to tell you." I watched as each of the players talked to Ron. The fight was over. I felt so tired, I wanted to fall into a deep sleep. I couldn't have gone out to celebrate, even if I'd wanted to. Years and years of looking for a home we could call our own had taken its toll. Rossen covered me up with a blanket and I closed my eyes. As the door shut behind the group, I could hear Lesley giggling away. "Now I know why we call her Gigglejuice," I thought to myself.

"Oops, we forgot Ted. He's still swimming," said Benny.

I must have slept for hours. The sun shining through the windows woke me up. I stretched a long stretch, standing on the tip of my toes, then collapsing to my knees. I made my way to the bathroom and turned on the shower. The water beating down on my face felt great. When the phone rang, I grabbed a towel and fought my way through the steam to the phone. I almost slipped on the bathroom floor reaching for the phone, which fell out of my hand. Soap was everywhere as I used the towel to wipe the receiver dry.

"Hello, Diane, it's Ron. You won't believe this." He sounded agitated. "The front page of Toronto's *Globe and Mail* broke the news that the city of Toronto has expropriated our building. The whole area is going to be redeveloped."

I thought I was dreaming. Confusion swelled inside my head. I sat on the toilet and cried.

4

Change
of Plans

"Okay, who was the asshole who thought it would be a great idea to show the Famous People Players a building they knew was going to be expropriated in the first place?" I said to the official in the planning department of the city of Toronto from my hotel room in Florida.

"Diane, I'm sorry. We couldn't tell you," he apologized.

"You didn't have to show it to me."

"Well, I, personally, didn't know about the expropriation."

"Wait a minute." My voice was getting louder. "You didn't know that the building you showed us, that you introduced us to, that was your big idea, that got everybody excited, that wasted the parents' and the architects' time, that shattered the dreams of the Famous People Players, was going to be expropriated?" I wanted to punch him right where it hurts! Lucky for him I was so far away.

"We're paying all the damages and the legal costs incurred by Famous People Players," he assured me. "We are all so very sorry. Honestly, Diane, I didn't know. But we are going to assume responsibility for this. We are going to relocate you and find you a new developer. We are going to give the developer a special density allowance to accommodate the Famous People Players. I promise you this. We won't let you down."

City officials found us a new location and a new developer. The location was on Wellington Street, right across from the SkyDome, where for us, the sky was the limit. The new developer was the Silver Mine Development Corporation.

I made a quick trip home, leaving Janet in charge of the Famous People Players.

"Don't worry, dear," said Ted at the airport. "Gord and I will take care of everything."

When I arrived, I met with a whole new set of players. The Silver Mine Development Corporation was proud to have Famous People Players join their family in a major development that would be a coup for Toronto.

"The Famous People Players will be smack in the middle of all the action downtown," the planners said. "You can attract all the people from the Blue Jays games to come to the theater."

I stood on the parking lot that was soon going to be our home, looking across at the SkyDome and imagining all the people walking across the street to see the Famous People Players.

"Stop daydreaming!" Judi snapped her fingers in front of my face. "There's lots to do if we're going to conduct a major capital campaign for the Famous People Players. For starters, we'll need a professional fundraising consultant, someone very experienced in capital campaign funding."

She explained that the government of Canada wouldn't consider an application for funding unless we had a feasibility study done, and for this we needed professional fundraising consultants. She mentioned a highly specialized firm that she had heard about.

"What the hell is a feasibility study and why does the government need it?" I asked.

"It's to determine if it will be financially possible to bring this project to fruition," explained Judi.

"*Of course* I'm going to bring the project to fruition! Why go to all the trouble of doing a study? I've studied this company for years; I don't need someone to ask me all kinds of questions and interview hundreds of people to see if I'm going to build a home for the company."

"Diane, wake up and smell the coffee. The government needs this study because they've funded so many projects in the past and then later found out that there wasn't enough financial support to continue with them."

"But I'm not going to do that. I'm going to see the project through to completion if it's the last thing I do."

"Diane, you have to prove that you have continuing funding in place and support in the community for this project. In other words, no ticket, no laundry. Just don't start screaming when I tell you that it will cost $45,000 to do the study."

"$45,000!" I screamed (how well Judi knows me). "Why so much money? Why does everything have to be so expensive, and who is going to pay for this?"

"You have to pay for this," Judi explained patiently, "because you are going to the government for the first time in years and asking for big bucks. You have to prove, as I said before, that this project is not going to be a financial disaster."

"I'm really confused. We don't *have* any money. That's why we are going to go out and fundraise. I can't believe they expect us to pay out that kind of money. Fundraising to me means that we don't have money and that's why we're asking for money. Spending money to prove that we need money doesn't make any sense to me."

"Diane, I could stand here all afternoon arguing about this with you, and I do understand how you feel, but when you construct a building, the first step is a feasibility study. Once the consultants complete the study, then we have to decide whether we want this same firm to do the capital campaign. This would be determined on the basis of the completed feasibility study, which will indicate whether they are able to get the funds necessary to complete the project. That is what we are paying $45,000 to learn. But I'm not finished yet, it gets worse. If we hire them to conduct this capital campaign, it's going to cost us." Judi paused and looked at me.

"How much, Schwartz, is this going to cost?"

"Well, that depends," she said slowly. "Why don't you sit down?"

"Why do I need to sit down?"

"Because if you don't, you will faint, and I'm not going to pick your body up off the ground."

"Okay." I went over to a bench and sat down. "I'm sitting down."

"It's going to cost $12,000 a month for one year to raise $3 million, because that is what you need to build a theater center for the Famous People Players."

"$12,000 a month! $12,000 a month!" I kept repeating. "You have to be joking."

"I'm not joking. Believe it or not, that is the going rate."

"How are we going to pay $12,000 for this service?"

"Well, I don't know, but when you think of it, once the money is raised for the building, it will be worth the investment. I suggest that we check out the firm I've mentioned. They can undertake the feasibility study and then, if it works out, they can handle the capital campaign. We can talk to some of our patrons who have worked with them on other projects and find out what their track record is."

We were advised by experienced people to hire the fundraisers immediately and to let the same group manage the feasibility study and the capital campaign. A bank manager told me, "We would consider coming on board to support your campaign only if you had a reputable fundraising consultant, and this firm is considered one of the best. They are expensive, but they're worth the $12,000-a-month retainer. You'll get it all back," he assured me. "Believe me, it will be your best investment. You'll get great returns for a $3-million capital campaign—it will end up costing Famous People Players only about $200,000. You have to invest money to make money."

Everywhere we went I was told that this company was the best in the business. They knew the people with the money. The powers that be and the people in the know said so, so it must be right. We decided to go ahead and in 1990 Judi and the board signed a contract with the consultants for a feasibility study to find out if the Famous People Players needed a home and if there was financial support in the community for the project.

I felt nervous about the expense of the study, and the night before I was due to meet the consultants, I tossed and turned for hours. I started to pray to Saint Jude, patron saint of hopeless causes. I figured that if it worked for Danny Thomas, the great comedian who dedicated his work to building hospitals for terminally ill patients, it would work for me. "Why is it," I wondered, "that we always pray when we're in trouble and not when everything is all right?" I finally fell asleep.

The next day I was anxious to get to my first meeting with our fundraising consultants. Their offices were certainly impressive: beautifully decorated and designed for comfort, quite a change from our warehouse with the orange crates I was using to sit on. They brought in fancy teas, coffee, and muffins. "You can't help but succeed in an environment like this one," I told myself. "Everything is all laid out for you, nice and easy." My gut kept saying, "Too easy," as I drank my Earl Grey tea, but I told my gut to shut up.

Over the next three months, the consultants interviewed fifty people and concluded that we did have support in the community and that we could raise the money. They even said that this would be a "relatively small capital campaign," although the budget looked enormous to me. They came up with a campaign strategy and something they called a "critical path" for soliciting $1.25 million from the private sector. It all sounded so brisk and professional and expert. I told my gut they were doing just fine.

Meanwhile, we were working around the clock to get ready for the ground-breaking ceremonies in June. The architectural drawings were under way and the designs looked exciting. The developer worked closely with our architect, Brisbin, Brook, Beynon, who I nicknamed the Busy Bees.

The consultants helped us with the preparations. Actually, when I say "helped," I am not being completely accurate. Although they had seemed professional about the details of the feasibility study, they didn't seem comfortable with the small details of organizing a special event. They kept making mistakes, or "kerfuffles," as the consultants called them. My gut had another name for them.

"Oh dear. Sorry, Diane. We've had another kerfuffle."

We had planned to invite quite a number of dignitaries to the ground-breaking ceremonies, including ministers from the federal and provincial governments. The invitations were to be hand-delivered by the players.

Lesley kept running into my office to show me how the consultants had mislabelled envelopes. "One's upside down, Diane," she pointed out. Giggle, giggle. Lesley Brown, or Gigglejuice, a cute blonde girl with one eye that shuts when she concentrates really hard, almost always begins her conversations with "What would you say if?"

"What would you say if I told you the label was on crooked?"

"What would you say if they forgot to put the invitation in the envelope?"

"What would you say if the word 'Shit' is written on the label?"

"What?" I screamed. "Let me see that!"

"They made a mistake," Lesley giggled. "What do you say about that?" she said, pointing to the envelope.

I couldn't believe that what I saw was a typing error. The words should have been "KeeWhit," but some idiot had actually typed "KeeShit." I picked up the phone, punching out the number with so much anger that I thought the buttons were going to jam.

"Get me Ms. Kerfuffle."

I imagined her in her lavish office, in the middle of something very important, like ordering croissants and muffins and special teas for our next meeting. She picked up the phone.

"I refuse to be responsible for proofreading!" I yelled at her. "That is not my job! You're a professional firm, you shouldn't make such mistakes."

Ms. Kerfuffle was sincerely sorry. "We'll fix it. We're so sorry, I'll speak to my assistant and tell her to be more careful. Oh dear, oh dear, I'm so sorry."

"I cannot be responsible for every dotted *i* or crossed *t* on an envelope," I told her before I hung up. My gut kept saying that these people were not right for us, but my brain kept saying firmly, "They are professionals, experts, and they've been highly recommended by everyone who knows about fundraising. This is just a fluke. They'll get on track soon." I took some more antacid to keep my gut quiet.

The ground-breaking ceremonies were almost upon us and everyone was anxious for the event to take place. It was our dream. "Please," I prayed, "please God, Saint Jude, and my Guardian Angel, let it go well."

"When will the contract be ready to sign?" I nervously asked Pat Anderson, our lawyer.

"Everything is ready, but the developer would like you to sign it on the day of the event. It will make a great picture for the press." I could hear my gut muttering darkly about "last-minute arrangements," but I didn't bother to listen.

"What are you going to wear?" asked Gigglejuice as she burst into my office.

I had no idea.

"What did you say when I reminded you?" Gigglejuice bragged. "What did you say about that?"

She stared at me intently. Terry and I grabbed our purses to go shopping. As I dashed to the car, I heard Gigglejuice yelling, "What would you say if I got your credit card for you? You forgot it. What would you say about that?"

"Lesley, you're too much," I laughed. "What would I ever do without you?"

"What would you say if I told you that me and Sandy delivered all the invitations ourselves? What would you say about that? What would you say if we trained Else ourselves to help us?"

"I'd say we should have hired you and Sandy to work on the capital campaign."

"Don't worry," she giggled. "It's gonna be all right. You worry too much."

That evening, I bought a suit and hat that could stop traffic. I was ready to dig a hole the size of a crater and put in the first floor. Now, if only I could get rid of those butterflies, I thought, as I punched my pillow to get a nice comfortable sleep. "Good night, Saint Jude, please let everything go well tomorrow." I went to sleep.

5

Ground-Breaking Day

Ground-breaking day. June 13, 1990. I leapt out of bed. I felt like a groundhog on Groundhog Day. And if you've ever seen the movie *Groundhog Day*, you'll know what I mean when I say that over the next six months, I really began to feel that it was Groundhog Day and I was Bill Murray.

I arrived at work to find Sandy Ciccone and Lesley waiting to see what I was going to wear. Debbie Rossen was on hand to help keep me organized, as I left a trail of bags, clothes, shoes, eye glasses, make-up, notes, papers, and my daily diary behind me.

"When we open our theater center," I told her, "we will put you in charge of Lost and Found." Debbie smiled. She was in charge of me and it made her feel great.

The phone rang. It was Joe Clark, minister of External Affairs and the former prime minister. At first, listening to his deep voice, I thought maybe it was Rich Little playing a joke on me, but his sincerity gave him away. It really was Joe.

"I wish I could be there with you and the group today to see that shovel go in the ground. Famous People Players are great Canadians and I'm very proud of all of you." My eyes started to well up, as everyone gathered around the phone to listen in. The call couldn't have come at a better time.

We felt confident when we arrived at the ground-breaking site. Our hearts were light and the players' faces were shinier than the new golden shovel that was soon to plunge into the ground. A huge crowd of fans, patrons, and passersby was gathering.

"Gosh, there must be at least two hundred people," said Benny.

The performers climbed up to a makeshift stage, which was filled with chairs for the ministers and dignitaries to sit on, and a podium for them to speak. Our life-size puppets of Anne Murray and Liberace were facing the cameras and waving to the audience.

As I looked around at all the smiles and faces, I spotted Pat Anderson. He beckoned me over. I rushed behind the platform, away from the crowd of friends and supporters, to meet him.

"Diane, the developers have played a dirty trick on us. They didn't sign the contract as promised," he whispered to me.

Jesus, Mary, and Joseph, please don't do this to me now, I prayed.

"They want us to sign an extra clause."

"What clause?" I was ready to kill the developer's representative, who was walking directly toward me. "You want to add what?" I yelled at him. My hat fell off.

He stood in front of me, but he couldn't look at me. "Diane, it's no big deal, honey. Trust me," he said. "It has to do with the fact——"

I cut him off. "I don't trust anybody who calls me honey. Where's your boss?"

"He's away on business. We want you to sign the following clause."

"Oh, how convenient. He's away on business." I snatched the contract from his hands and started to read.

The parties acknowledge and agree that this Offer to Lease and the agreement arising upon its acceptance is terminable at the option of either party, acting in its respective sole and unfettered discretion, until 5:00 p.m. on November 15, 1990. In the event that either party provides written notice to other party on or before 5:00 p.m. on November 15, 1990, that it is exercising its right to terminate this Offer to Lease and the agreement arising upon its acceptance, all of the rights and obligations of the parties shall become null and void and of no force and effect and neither party shall have any liability to the other.

"You mean to say that your boss sent you here with this amendment to our contract on the day of our ground-breaking ceremonies, with all of the press and the ministers here to watch? This is a scam." I burst into tears. All these people, the press, the politicians, our friends, the performers—my God, the performers! This will break their hearts, I thought.

Pat tried to calm me down so that the crowd of people wouldn't notice something was wrong. Ivan Fleischmann could see I was upset and rushed over to prevent me from taking a swing at someone. I showed him the revised contract.

"What do I do? Do I tell them the wedding is off? What announcement should I make?" I asked him as Gord Swayze, a member of our board of directors, and Pat talked things over with the developer's representative. Their conversation faded away and I was left alone with my inner voice.

"I'm in trouble," I thought, "because I listened to too many people and didn't listen to the one most important person, me, my gut. Dear God, please tell me what to do. If I announce that it's over to all these people, I will publicly throw the whole capital campaign into serious jeopardy." I looked around at the crowd. I noticed the wonderful pride in the eyes of the parents, the staff, the performers, and all our friends. Even Ms. Kerfuffle and her staff were proud to be there on this great day. I took a deep breath and asked my gut for the answer.

"Go for it, Diane. Take the risk, it will work out. You've got to have faith," my inner voice said. I turned to Gord and Pat.

"We'll go through with the ceremonies as planned," I said. I felt sick. "We will sign the lease with the clause as you requested," I told the developer's representative, but I wanted to smack him. "Mr. All-Talk, you tell Mr. No-Action that if anything goes wrong and the Famous People Players are hurt in any way, you will have me personally to contend with, and the law firm of Finagle, Finagle and Swindle will have one hell of a fight on their hands."

I put my hat back on and returned to the platform, shaking slightly. I almost caught my heel between the boards that held the platform together. As I walked toward the microphone and looked around at all the eyes staring at me, my hands were sweating and my heart was pounding in my throat. But when I started to speak, a sudden feeling of calmness came over me. My heart stopped pounding and my hands started to move.

"It has long been a dream of ours to have our own home in downtown Toronto, and no matter how many disappointments and frustrations we've had, no matter how many major setbacks we've encountered, we've never let go of the dream.

"The Famous People Players are a remarkable group of people who create the magic that weaves lessons of life inside me. They continue to show me that if you dare to dream, dare to believe, your dreams can come true.

"No matter what success we achieved, we often learned that there was a price to pay for the glimpse of stardust we touched: going to Broadway, visiting the Great Wall of China, sharing the same stage for ten years with our dear friend Liberace. We've lost members and trained new members, and through it all we never let go of our dream, that one day we'd have a place we could call our very own Emerald City.

"To all of the Famous People Players who are here today, I thank you for being the wind that pushed me to fly."

I introduced them one at a time: Benny D'Onofrio, Debbie Lim, Debbie Rossen, Ted and Gord Billinger, Else Buck, Lisa Tuckwell, Darlene Arsenault, Greg Kozak, Sandra Ciccone, Lesley Brown, Michelle Busby, Charleen Clarke, and all the wonderful staff, including my mother, Mary Thornton, her two brilliant prop artists Therese Picco and Enrico Basco, and my right arm, Terry Paterson.

"So here we are today, dreaming again about a home for the Famous People Players. Today we start to raise $3 million to make it all happen, and it will happen."

The audience cheered. I turned to the government officials who were representing the prime minister and Hugh O'Neil from the provincial government.

"I hope, Mr. Ministers, that you will take this message back to the prime minister and the premier of Ontario: that we should stop calling it the Ministry for Disabled Persons, and call it the Ministry for People who are Disabled, because we are people first, disabled second."

The applause was enormous and both the ministers smiled at each other, as they were given their new mandate.

We took the shovel with the support of Hugh O'Neil, minister of Culture and Communications, who had shocked the crowd into hysterical applause with his pledge of $1 million to our dream. I felt I had made the right decision.

6

"The Lieutenant Governor of Canada"

I take my commitment, my word to someone, as gospel. When I say I'm going to do something, by golly, I do it. It's the same for Famous People Players. When we sign a contract for a performance, we deliver a performance. We bust our asses to get to one destination after another, no matter what troubles we meet along the way. It doesn't matter if hail, storms, or tornados get in our way, the show must go on. We deliver and we take pride in our delivery.

The world is full of people who don't feel that pride, and worse, don't dream. Dreams are so important, particularly when everything is gloomy with the recession. We must go inward and find that dream that we put away and never realized. But everyone is full of excuses. It will never happen because I'm too old, or because I don't have enough money. One excuse after another. We procrastinate and put our dreams on the back burner. We whine about injustice, unfairness, but do we ever do anything about it? No, because we just don't have the guts, and it takes guts to dream and dream big. It takes even more guts to go from one dream to another.

It's through triumph over adversity that we succeed. Michael Jordan was dropped from his grade nine basketball team, but he had a dream. Walt Disney had several setbacks and failures, but he had a dream. José Feliciano lived with his seven brothers and sisters in one room in extreme poverty in Puerto Rico, but he had a dream. Thomas Edison tried hundreds of light bulbs that didn't work, but he had a dream.

By all rights, Famous People Players shouldn't have seen its nineteenth year, but we had a dream.

We had our share of adversity too. I came face to face with it on one of our tours. The bus, filled with laughing excited players, left Toronto to take the Famous People Players on a major United States tour that would start in California. I had too much fundraising work to do, so I had planned to catch up with the players at their first performance in Los Angeles.

"Don't worry," said Else, shaking as she carried her suitcase onto the bus.

"Yeah, boss," said Gord, "you've got Teddy and me to look after everything."

Janet, the stage manager, led the tour to California. The bus let them off at a motel in Los Angeles. Everyone was so tired from the five-day bus ride that all they wanted to do was go to their rooms and lie down. But Janet insisted everyone go for a short walk to get some exercise before heading out to dinner. It wasn't a great area to walk, near an exit ramp off the highway. California is designed for cars, not pedestrians.

Janet, briskly walking ahead of everyone, stopped at the crosswalk. A drunk driver ran the red light, slammed into another car and forced it onto the sidewalk, where it knocked Janet down.

Some of the performers can still hear the sound of the shattering glass.

"Janet's in hospital," Ted and Gord cried to me on the phone.

"Come quick, we need you," said Benny.

Kamile Smith, one of our staff performers, rose to the occasion and took charge. "Don't worry about the company, everything is under control. We will stay at the hospital with Janet until you arrive."

My mother and I took the first flight to Los Angeles and rushed to the hospital to find Janet lying there unable to speak or move. The performers waiting outside intensive care were shocked. It was hard for us to see Janet in this condition. She had always been so active, running back and forth on stage, loading and unloading the props. She was so strong, yet there she lay, unable to walk, strapped to a board.

We never know from one day to the next what lies in store for us, what hand is dealt to us by life.

Phil Chart, our truck driver, and a real rock and roller, quickly assumed the position of stage manager as the players continued the tour. Janet was flown back to Toronto, where she went into rehabilitation to learn to walk again. It was a tragedy for a strong and active woman like her, and a blow to the Famous People Players. Yet we had to carry on.

As we had planned, we contracted with the same fundraising firm that had done the feasibility study to have them create, manage, and execute a successful campaign for the Famous People Players. But my gut wasn't at all happy. I was worried about meeting the $12,000-a-month payment to them, the largest fee I had ever paid in my life. I was worried enough about how on earth I was going to pay the rent, the salaries, the telephone bills, and the cost of props and transportation for the company tours.

I was so scared that I couldn't sleep the night after I signed the contract. I tossed and turned, worrying about the future and the livelihood of each of the players. Counting sheep was no good, as I kept seeing the faces of Ted, Gord, Benny, and Debbie Lim as they jumped over fences. They trusted me with their lives. I couldn't let them down.

"This firm has to raise the money," I thought. "Then it will be worth the investment. Please, Saint Jude, let it all work out."

We all met in the fundraisers' office, waiting to get the professionals' directions to the quickest and simplest way to reach our destination safely. "We are so excited," the consultants gushed. "We love Famous People Players and this is going to be a fun project for us. Three million will be a snap to raise. The federal government should

give $500,000, the province $1 million, and we'll raise $1.5 million.
The banks have a formula that they go by, they usually give only 1
per cent of the total private-sector goal, but because this is such a
small campaign, they will probably make an exception to the rule.
The bank you do business with should contribute $100,000 and oth-
ers should follow. They always watch each other and do what your
bank does."

Looking straight at me, they stood confident and firm.

"Great. Let's get some appointments to see the CEOs and start
banking the money for the building fund," I said.

The first meeting had got off to a good start, and members of
my board were impressed. "We've made the right decision," said Ron
Secker.

That night I slept better. Thank you, Saint Jude.

I spent the next couple of days trying to get the CEOs to see me.
"We need door openers," our consultants said. "Let's get going."

"For $12,000 a month," my gut said, "they should get the appoint-
ments," but I didn't say this aloud.

I convinced one great banker, Hart MacDougall, to help us.
"All I want you to do," I said, "is ask them to see me for just fifteen
minutes." It won't take long, I thought, to get the money.

It was quite an experience seeing how the CEOs of our major
banks conducted business. Their offices were unbelievable. I marveled
at the expensive paintings on the walls, the antique furniture, the spa-
ciousness. The offices were like palaces. One in particular made me
feel as though I was in a James Bond movie. The security was unbelievable. One door after another kept opening, probably twelve in all,
until I reached the CEO's office. It reminded me of the credit sequence
of the "Get Smart" television series.

They listened, they all listened. Some had tons of questions about
the company, others were non-committal and quiet. One CEO shook
my hand fast and sat me down in his grand office. He turned his
clock on and timed me.

"I have five minutes," he said briskly.

Talking as fast as I could, I described the dream to him. I told him how much we needed his bank's contribution and waited for a response. He thanked me politely and that was that. In other words, don't call us, we'll call you. On my way out, I decided I was glad that Famous People Players was doing business with another bank.

Our roller-coaster was hurtling downward. We had a change of provincial government in Ontario. Hugh O'Neil of the Liberal Party, our greatest supporter, was no longer the minister of Culture and Communications. We had a new premier, Bob Rae, and a new party in power, the New Democratic Party. We lost the $1-million pledge from the province and some of our corporate pledges. Several of the Canadian corporations that had promised us money were crumbling before our eyes. I was scared. We needed $3 million. The federal government's commitment was $500,000 and I had raised close to $300,000. Without money from the province, we were in serious trouble.

We also organized a gala, although we did this by ourselves, without the help of the consultants. Steve Kroft from "60 Minutes" came up to join us, and so did Leslie Nielsen. Leslie is one of Canada's greatest comedians. We'd first met years before, when he toured with us and acted as our narrator. At the gala, he reminisced about that tour. "Never forget your roots," he said to us. "I know how hard you all work. I know what it's like to set up in a new theater each night, perform, then strike the set and travel to your next stop, all in forty-below weather. I did that with you, but remember that the hard work you do makes the world a better place. And, yes, there is life after Famous People Players." Everyone laughed, because his career had really taken off afterward when he starred in the movie *The Naked Gun*.

Meanwhile, back at the fundraising firm, things were slowing down. Each meeting was a repeat of the last meeting. The consultants continued to sound positive and confident, but nothing ever seemed to happen. I began to refer to them as Smoke and Mirrors Ltd.

Smoke and Mirrors left everything to the last minute. They had six weeks' notice to set up appointments for me to visit the head offices of major corporations. But good old Ms. Kerfuffle, assisted by her staff, kept trying to arrange appointments just a couple of days in advance.

We were constantly dropping what we were doing to help them. Terry Paterson frequently had to leave her post to run over to their offices to recover important documents that they couldn't find in their computer files. The wrong letters were sent to the wrong donors. I wrote to my board: "Ms. Kerfuffle, of Smoke and Mirrors Ltd., lacks overall direction and supervision of her staff." Our office was constantly faxing, proofreading, and editing their work. We were exhausted.

Staff came and went at Smoke and Mirrors. I never knew who I would be talking to from one day to the next. Finally I yelled, "Stop this merry-go-round! I want to get off!" But I was advised not to change the arrangements. "If you fire your campaign counsellors, a red light is set off in the corporate world," I was told. "People will think the campaign is in trouble. Nobody wants to be part of a flop, it would be most damaging to everyone's reputation. Keep them on, ride them hard, supervise them, and don't let them out of your sight." I couldn't believe it, but this was the advice given to me by many of our devoted contributors.

My stomach was in knots. If I dared to take an aspirin, my butterflies would use it as a ping-pong ball. We got to the point where their secretary would write out a proposal and expect us to type it. I was furious. We were paying them $12,000 a month and they had the nerve to ask us to type up their proposals! I was spitting mad. My eyes were spinning with anger, my hair was standing on end. The stress gave me constipation, while I had diarrhea of the mouth.

Smoke and Mirrors even dared to criticize the members of my board. They said, "Your chairman is not blue-blooded enough. You need people from Who's Who to open doors. The name alone should bring in the money."

I couldn't believe what I was hearing. Charles Tisdall, our chairman, was incredibly dedicated and so were other members, like Judi Schwartz and Gordon Swayze. They had worked hard for years to help me realize our dream. No amount of "blue blood" could replace their commitment. I wasn't about to find a new board.

An elaborate brochure was proposed that would express our dream to the potential benefactors. A photographer took some wonderful pictures of Benny holding a puppet of Superman, the company in rehearsal, performers traveling on the subway, and company members learning to cook. The brochure was supposed to describe our plans for a state-of-the-art complex where young people with disabilities could come and join the Famous People Players and be part of the dream.

Ms. Kerfuffle recommended a firm that would design and produce the brochure. Two creative professionals came to Famous People Players to discuss the layout of the brochure. They gave all kinds of instructions to do this and that, without so much as a please or thank you.

I have great difficulty with people who don't want to listen to anyone else's thoughts and ideas. Even if my ideas were wrong, the attitude they displayed was very condescending to the staff of Famous People Players and they didn't give us the respect I thought we deserved.

This was not the first time this had happened to us and, unfortunately, it wouldn't be the last. I guess so-called normal people have this abnormal quality in them. They have a superiority complex. Some people have real difficulty being in an environment like ours. There is too much honesty floating around at Famous People Players. All of us say what's on our minds and we aren't ashamed of what we feel.

The performers do not use their minds to discover their way in life, they use their souls to express how they feel. They are not ashamed to cry in public, or to stand up in a crowd and say "I need help;" "I'm lost;" "I can't read;""I'm still a virgin at thirty-three." Unlike the so-called normal people, they listen to their souls speak to them every day.

Terry and I watched uncomfortably as the professionals created their masterpiece. In the boardroom of Smoke and Mirrors, they discussed their ideas among themselves, ignoring Terry and me.

Finally, they presented a draft to us. It was stunning, with one minor exception.

"I want the message that I wrote put back the way I wrote it," I said.

They all looked at each other, not at me, and started to discuss with each other what to do.

I had written:

The Famous People Players theater center will be the first in the world to offer life skills training and counselling to people with disabilities as part of the regular operations of a professional performance company.

"Hello? Remember me down here at the other end of the table, the paying customer? I'm the client. I hired you. Now please change the message."

I could read their thoughts behind their smiles as they agreed to comply with my wishes. They couldn't stand me.

"Famous People Players are paying your firm a fortune, need I remind you."

The message was changed, and five thousand brochures were printed. They were to arrive at our doorstep Monday morning.

The box arrived on schedule. We opened it and admired how beautifully and exquisitely the brochure had been produced. Gorgeous, I thought, absolutely gorgeous. Now everyone will take us seriously.

Then I started to read the list of patrons on the inside cover. I let out a scream. There it was, the blooper to end all bloopers. "The Honourable Lincoln Alexander, Lieutenant Governor of Canada." Not Ontario, but Canada. What an embarrassment. Imagine calling an American state governor "Governor of the United States of America." I did a hundred-yard dash to the phone and started yelling at the poor receptionist at Smoke and Mirrors.

"Get me Ms. Kerfuffle."

"She isn't in. She's getting her hair done."

"Find her and get her to call me. Tell her her artsy-fartsy brochure people called Ontario's lieutenant governor 'the lieutenant governor of Canada.'"

I slammed the phone down and picked it up just as fast to dial Ron.

"Wait till you see it!" I was hysterical. "This has to stop, Ron. We have no money and all the money we are spending is being wasted."

Ron couldn't agree with me more. "They have to go."

Just after I hung up the phone, Terry came into my office with an envelope in her hands.

"Diane, it gets worse. Their bill for the brochure went over budget by $10,000." It had ended up costing $28,000.

"Do people think we're rich or something? What image do we have out there that people think they can continue to rip us off? Well, they're in for a big surprise."

As I waited for the phone to ring, I paced like a panther waiting to kill.

Finally, Ms. Kerfuffle got on the phone to me, crying.

"We're so sorry. We can fix it and we will pay for it."

"Look, for this kind of money, you shouldn't have to fix anything. We shouldn't *be* in this situation. You should have supervised this more carefully. It blows my mind how unprofessional you people are. Doesn't anybody there have a conscience? When a corporation asks me to produce a performance, they want to know up front how much it will cost and how long it will take. I tell them, for instance, it will take two months and $50,000. I enter into a contract with the sponsoring body. Perhaps after I've signed it, I find out that it's really going to take four months, therefore I need another $50,000. Well, guess what, Ms. Kerfuffle? That's *my* problem. I have to deliver a show and I'm responsible for fulfilling those contracts even if it costs me money. That is what integrity in business is all about. I guess the point I'm making is that we entered into a contract with your company in good faith, expecting to work in harmony with people who are experts in capital campaign funding. I would be less than honest not to express our great disappointment and hurt that the money we have spent, which we earned through our performances, has shown no return to date. I will be calling a board meeting, and you will be hearing from our lawyer. Meanwhile, you will get that brochure fixed and, as you said, you will pay for it. As for the difference in price, you can pay for that too." I hung up.

"You're not getting off the hook that easy." I looked up to see my mother standing beside my desk. My heart jumped—I hoped she hadn't heard me. "If she ever finds out about what we have gotten ourselves into with our fundraising consultants, she will kill me," I thought.

"Your lease is up. Can you pay the increase for this rat-infested warehouse?" She looked down at me.

"How much do they want?"

"Another $1,500 a month." Her strong arms folded into one another.

"$1,500!" My heart skipped a beat. Or three.

"They should give it to us for free for all the extra tenants we have living with us." I said. "Therese and I took the wall apart by the rehearsal room to find another rat and her babies poisoned to death from stuff we had left out for them last night." I slumped in my chair.

"I don't know why you're collapsing," Mary said. "We're the suckers who cleaned up this mess."

"Let's just go," I said. "I'll tell them we're not renewing the lease."

"And let's try once again to report them to the health board," Mary suggested.

"The health board!" I screamed. "That's City Hall! The bureaucracy, the red tape! Forget it. Time is money. Let's just look for a new place."

"We have exactly one month," Mary said. She turned to Therese, her assistant. "Get Enrico, we'll drive to some of the buildings advertised for lease."

Mary shuffled out of my office in her slippers, which were ripped at the seams. I called Judi on the phone and started to tell her about the rats, the lease, and the other problems that I was dealing with.

"I'm exhausted by all these setbacks. I'm just about ready to check myself into the Queen St. mental hospital," I sighed into the phone.

"Mary will find something, she always does," Judi reassured me.

"We're broke. We can't keep paying this fee to a firm that continues to screw up everything. The straw that broke the camel's back for me was the brochures."

"You have a contract," she insisted. "It's up soon. Let's ride it out. If you want to find someone else to take over from you, so you don't have to deal with Smoke and Mirrors, go right ahead. Get someone with a new outlook."

I wasn't sure how I could get out. There was too much clean-up work to be done. The government grants that they had initiated needed lots of work. Plus, the government wanted another feasibility study, this time on the designs itself, before we would get any money, Judi told me. I couldn't delegate the job of dealing with Smoke and Mirrors to anyone else. But I couldn't take the stress anymore. We needed help.

7

A New
Angel in
Our Lives

Judi was right, we needed someone with a fresh outlook.

I remembered with fondness a wonderful woman, Thelma Wells, whom I'd met in Austin, Texas. She'd been in the communications department at IBM when I'd been their keynote speaker at a conference. It had been one of the most enjoyable weeks of my life. We'd got along like a house on fire and she had a great sense of humor. I knew she'd be the perfect person to help us make the transition from Smoke and Mirrors back to Famous People Players. I decided to get in touch with her.

Meanwhile, after a week of searching, Mary had come up with a place that we could temporarily call home. It was another warehouse in downtown Toronto, in an industrial district south of Queen Street West. It was not much different from the one we were in, except that it was bigger. There were lots of pillars holding up the weak ceiling and the ventilation was poor.

"It's as hot as an oven in here. We can't breathe," I said.

"Look, Dora Doom," my mother said angrily, "the landlords are excited to have the Famous People Players in their building. They are going to give it to us for the same rent as the one we're in now, and

it's twice the size of our old place! Do you have any better ideas?"
She glared at me.

Before I had a chance to respond, she was already orchestrating
the big move. "Remember, it's only temporary until we find a new
home," she said as she carried out a huge box of paints.

Shortly after we had moved into our temporary hothouse, I was
able to convince Thelma to come to Canada. Her love for the Famous
People Players was sincere. She was committed to our dream and
wanted to see it realized as badly as I did. It didn't take much coaxing
to get her on the next flight to Canada.

We all went to meet her at the airport. As soon as she got off the
plane, everyone in the Famous People Players ran to greet her.

"Remember me?" Benny said, as he picked up her suitcases.

"We need a bigger van to put all her stuff in," said Lesley, giggling
away. "How much stuff did you bring?"

"Well, I didn't know what the weather was like up here and all,"
Thelma said in her Texas drawl.

We drove her to Mary's, her home for the next few months.

Thelma and I spent hours catching up on news and gossip. Just
having her around made me feel more confident. As my mother put
it: "God works in mysterious ways, and here we are with a new angel
in our lives, Thelma Wells."

Thelma rolled up her sleeves and got to work right away. She
gathered the staff at the fundraising office and announced that she
was now the project manager. Their faces dropped.

"Diane will be working with the Famous People Players. It will
be my job to ensure that this transition with the government feasibility studies and corporations goes smoothly for both sides. My
expertise is in the field of communications and I'm sure I will be an
asset to the project," she said firmly.

After a year and a half of delays and "kerfuffles," including an extra
six months during which we had to renew their contract at half-
price to get the job finished, Thelma managed the transition wonderfully. Soon we had all the files back in our office, and we parted

company with Smoke and Mirrors remarkably cordially. I was never more relieved to get out of a situation in my life. Count your blessings, write off your losses, and go forward, I told myself.

With Thelma's know-how and guidance to help us, we were able to work beautifully together, even if we had to reinvent the wheel. But this was a wheel that would move smoothly down our yellow brick road, with no blowouts. Terry and I found it easy to work with Thelma. Our ideas clicked. Good things were happening to the Famous People Players. I was able to go on tour knowing that Terry and Thelma had everything under control. Letters wouldn't be sent out with the wrong labels or mistyped addresses. There would be no mismanagement of any kind.

I had learned a valuable lesson in all of this. When you stop thinking of yourself and think of others, you can achieve anything. The people at Smoke and Mirrors were not interested in the Famous People Players, they were interested only in that $12,000 a month. The dream wasn't important to them, nor did they care how hard we worked to earn the money to pay them. That was the greedy 1980s. That decade turned people into selfish beings, putting themselves before others. Strange as it may sound, I was glad that it ended in a recession, because the recession brought us to our knees. We had to redeem ourselves in order to survive.

The board and I had to assume responsibility for everything that had gone wrong on the capital campaign. After all, the buck has to stop somewhere and it stopped with us. The money raised to help pay for the expenses of the campaign came not only from my speaking engagements, but also from the company's hard work performing at Sea World in Orlando, Florida.

As the leader, I feel a strong sense of responsibility, and it upsets me when money is wasted or badly invested. When this happens I feel I need to rectify the damage by creating a positive experience that enables us to grow stronger. And there were many positive aspects of the experience to think about.

For one thing, I had learned more about the caliber of the people around me. You are only as good as the people who work for you, and the people who work at Famous People Players are a dedicated group. They go far beyond the call of duty. Some may be green, but they all have hearts of gold. They are caring people who give of their time, doing everything from scrubbing floors and urinals to driving to fundraising. They do it because they believe in the company, the people, and the cause.

You always find out what people are really made of when they are faced with a challenge. Over and over again, the people who work with Famous People Players—the parents, the volunteers, the staff, the board of directors—show their true colors as they forgive, laugh mistakes off, and give everyone the benefit of the doubt. They do what they do because they love it. No one is motivated by money, all are motivated by the desire to strengthen the human spirit.

Throughout the years of searching for a home, I kept hearing the same comments over and over: "Nobody wants a theater company for people with special needs." "Nobody wants to be waited on by a handicapped person." "You have to spend lots of money on advertising and marketing to make it work." "You have to get the society people on board, the élite. They are the only ones who can make the project happen." "You have to get rid of your working board; they are not members of the élite. Their names mean nothing to anyone."

All these comments depressed me. And all of them were just plain wrong. And as for my board of directors, they stood by me in good times and bad. When the going got tough, they got going. Just because using the élite worked for other groups didn't mean it would work for us. Just because that is the way it has always been done doesn't mean that it's the way it should be done. I keep thinking of something Paul Newman once said: "If we ever have a plan, we're screwed!"

Going outside the company and paying the experts who had done this before to advise us and guide us was not a complete disaster or a waste of money, because we learned from the experience and that gave us the confidence to go forward with our dream, and to find out that we were the experts all along. We were the ones with the answers, because we were driven from the heart.

Terry and Thelma worked under unbelievably bad conditions. Unlike the Smoke and Mirrors staff, with their magnificent boardroom and their state-of-the-art equipment and lighting, we were working in a slum. The lightbulbs were burned out, the ceiling leaked. The warehouse was like a furnace in the summertime, and in the wintertime we never took our coats and gloves off because it was so cold.

But somehow, despite these conditions, we were able to revive the campaign on our own. Thelma set up appointments for corporate representatives to join the Famous People Players for a specially prepared lunch. Everyone took part in the dream. Mary showed the performers how to make lasagna. We set up tables and decorated the room. We were determined to sell our own campaign with our own road map. Everyone who came to visit us in our humble surroundings went away sold on our dream. They loved the food, and loved the way Gord and Benny acted as our maître d's at all the meetings we conducted from our home base.

"We did it," said Gigglejuice, giggling away to herself. "What would you say that me and Sandy made the lasagna today? What do you have to say about that? What would you say that I showed Else how to set the table? Well, what would you say about that?"

The recession hit us hard. Some theaters in the United States went under. Then the Gulf War broke out, which meant that a lot of people in the States did not want to be in public places for fear of bomb threats. A tour of California was canceled because of the 1992 Los Angeles riots. We lost a great summer gig at Knotts Berry Farms. The tourist industry suffered badly as conventions were canceled and people stayed home. Even theme parks were losing money. We lost a large part of our audience and ran up our first deficit ever.

Life on Highway 95, the road to Florida, was depressing. As we drove from city to city, performing to dwindling audiences, the news seemed to get worse and worse.

One day the bus stopped for us to have lunch at a Howard Johnson. Everyone got out and stretched their tired bodies from sitting so long. I went to a pay phone to call the office and see how Thelma and Terry were getting on. The phone rang three times, then I heard Terry's voice.

"Good afternoon, Famous People Players."

"Hi, it's me," I said. "How's everything going?"

"Can you speak a little louder?" Terry replied. "I can't hear you over the noise."

The truckers behind me were carrying on a loud conversation as the cash register beside me rang up one sale after another of junk food.

"How's everything going?" I yelled into the phone.

"The campaign has slowed down quite a bit, and business after business is going under. The news is awful." Terry sounded tired. "We're losing our pledges."

"Oh, Terry, come on, how bad can it be?"

"Look Diane, we're not farting in silk."

"We've got to stay positive and hopeful," I said. "I have to go. Rossen is calling me to get off the phone, our table is ready. I'll call after the first show tonight." I hung up.

That night the theater wasn't full. The feeling in the air was tense. The audience itself felt down. We had to lift their spirits.

It reminded me of the time we had worked with Tony Orlando. He'd come into our dressing room and said, "We're clowns, guys. We have to go out and make these people laugh and be happy. That's our job. You never know who's just lost their job, been dumped by their girlfriend or boyfriend, had a fight with their parents, or lost a lot of money. So for the next two hours, make them forget all their problems, and the problems of the outside world."

It was true. Laughter was the only cure for our problems. We had to laugh more and laugh hard. It seemed that whenever I went to see an executive of a corporation to ask for money for our building fund, their facial expressions were terminally professional. These people desperately needed to laugh.

I was also reminded of the time we had worked with Red Skelton. We were once his special guest stars on a television special for Home Box Office called "Funny Faces." We performed "Send in the Clowns," a number that I have always found particularly endearing.

The stage was set with two balloon stands. A small clown with a big red nose and big feet entered carrying a suitcase. Red loved this little clown. A tightrope appeared over his head and he looked up at it, wondering how he was going to get up there. The clown opened his suitcase and out came a bunch of moths. At that point we heard Red laughing in the wings. Suddenly, out came a big red balloon, which floated up toward the tightrope. The little clown grabbed its string and floated up with it.

The clown landed on the rope. He struggled hard to keep his position. He'd fall, then catch his nose on the rope. He'd struggle back, fall again, and catch his foot. We heard Red in the wings saying, "Come on, you can do it." Finally, just like magic, the clown got up and walked right across the rope. The studio audience and Red went wild.

Meeting Red Skelton during the taping of that show was such a joy. For years I had watched him on television doing one silly prank after another.

"I'll never forget the skit with the girdle," I told him.

"Hey, I still do that."

Right then and there he pretended he was a woman putting on a girdle. We howled with laughter, watching him as he twisted and turned to get into the imaginary girdle. He laughed harder than any of us.

"That's why I'm still around," he said. "I'm still young because I laugh at my own jokes all the time. Sometimes I laugh so hard that I have trouble getting to the punch line."

Red was right. We have to laugh. Look at George Burns, who lived to be one hundred years old. Look at Bob Hope, Milton Berle, and Victor Borge. They're all laughing and they're all still around.

I decided that difficult as this recession was for everyone, I had to keep laughing, because without laughter, without keeping my sense of humor, I would never find a home for the Famous People Players. That night, despite the small audience, we did our best to get the audience laughing. I hope that some of them there did forget their troubles for a couple of hours.

During the tour, I continually faxed Pat and Ron, asking them how the developers were holding up in the recession.

"I wish I was dealing with the Reichmanns, who are sound and credible," I wrote. "We're dealing with Mr. All-Talk and Mr. No-Action, and that scares me a lot. We've collected a lot of money from our campaign and I don't want to lose it or be forced to return it because we didn't build our theater center when we said we were going to build it."

Pat's response was a great relief.

"I spoke to the Silver Mine Development Corporation today. Everything is fine, I'm 100 per cent confident. Don't worry. They have leased space in the development to Imex, a hotel, restaurant, and some retail stores. There will be a delay on the construction, because the hotel hasn't completed its designs yet and Silver Mine is waiting for the recession to end, but it will go ahead in the end."

I was somewhat relieved, but I still felt a tight knot in my stomach that wouldn't go away. I kept wishing I had gone to the Reichmann brothers. I was sure we'd have been safe there.

The bus moved on down the road, our home for the time being.

"Diane, I got you your favorite newspaper and a cup of coffee," said Ted as he ran toward me. Each morning I knew I could count on Ted to bring me *U.S.A. Today*, a great newspaper to read on the road.

I settled into my seat on the bus and gave directions to the bus driver.

"Let's drive for four hours, then stop for lunch. Is that okay with everyone?" I yelled toward the back of the bus.

"As long as we can stop at Bob Evans's. I love their burgers," Benny yelled back.

Before I started reading the paper, I walked around the bus to have my morning chat with each of the players.

"Last night I watched a rerun of 'Dallas,'" Darlene said. "You should have seen what J.R. did to Sue Ellen."

"What did he do?"

"Oh, man, it was something, it was awful." She started to laugh.

"Tell me what happened."

But Darlene couldn't tell me. She wanted to, but she has a problem explaining what she sees. We've never figured out why she has this problem, but as long as she enjoys watching her soaps, that's all that matters.

"I love my soaps," Darlene said. "I just wish I could see 'The Young and the Restless.' I miss that," she said, as she looked at all the soap magazines she had picked up at truck stops.

I moved on down the aisle of the bus. Sandra, her head on her pillow, was trying to get some sleep.

"Up late, were we?"

"It was Gord. He had his TV on loud all night. I banged on the wall. I called to him in his room, but he wouldn't stop. All night, I tell you."

She put her head back on the pillow and closed her eyes. I looked over at Gord, who slid down in his seat and put his blanket over his head to avoid talking to me.

"Gord." I pulled the blanket down. "Guess what? It's morning and I want you to come and sit down at the front of the bus with me and make sure the bus is going in the right direction."

"But I'm tired, Diane."

"Too bad, Gord. You will keep your eyes open and tonight there will be no TV."

Gord got up and everyone applauded. Benny threw a paper cup at him, hitting him on the head.

"Okay, I apologize," he said. "It won't happen again."

"It'd better not," said Debbie Lim, who was knitting a sweater as Rossen held the wool for her.

Gord sat down across from Else and Gigglejuice Lesley, who were playing a game of cards. I took one last look around and noticed the staff were helping Greg and Michelle write postcards to their families.

"Else is doing real good," Lesley told me as I sat down again.

"I didn't drop my prop," Else said as she looked at me.

"I was very proud of you in the show last night. You held on to that fish, and I watched you move it right across the stage, just like a real fish."

She smiled. "I promise I won't shake. I'm trying."

"We know you're trying," said Rossen, "but why do you shake?"

"I don't know." She shook her head.

"Her key fell out of her hand last night. I helped her open her hotel room," Debbie Lim added.

It's like the blind leading the blind, I thought, as I took the lid off my coffee, but maybe the blind don't make such bad leaders after all. I put my feet up and took my first sip. Looking out the window, I thought what a great day it was. The sun was shining and the desert was beautiful. We were heading toward Arizona, my favorite state, where, in my teenage years, I'd done a lot of painful growing up.

I started to reflect on memories of my life in the 1960s, of traveling around in a beat-up station-wagon with my father through the hot desert, watching the cacti and stopping in small towns. That was a great time for me, even though Dad often put my tolerance and love to the test. My dad used to say his job as a parent was to protect, while my job as a child was to explore and seek adventure.

I could see his face superimposed on the Arizona canyons as we drove along and the rocks started to turn red with the changing light. My dad was a cowboy at heart, this was where his soul roamed. I wish he'd lived long enough to see what became of me and what I ended up doing with my life. He'd have been so proud. It's funny, but as I grow older I don't have any regrets. His harsh words and his anger made me stronger, and for that I'm truly grateful.

I picked up the newspaper and turned to the entertainment section. Sipping my coffee, I glanced over at Gord, whose head was nodding.

"Gord! Wake up and keep watching the road."

Gord shook his head and smiled at me.

"I'll watch Gord," said Rossen.

She gave the ball of wool to Else to take over for her and moved to sit beside Gord. It was funny, I thought, watching Rossen watch Gord watch the highway as it twisted and turned toward our destination.

I put down the paper and finished my coffee. For some reason I didn't feel like reading the news that day. It was time to meditate, my inner voice was saying. I put my head back, looked out the window, and watched the scenery go by. It looked as if all the cacti were waving hello to the Famous People Players. Break a leg, the cacti said to all of us. They were blessing the bus as we went by.

As the road began to climb, I looked down and saw a river rushing past. I imagined myself galloping alongside on my white horse, Silver, trying to race the river, moving with the wind in my hair and my horse panting hard to get me to my destination. At the end of the river would be Emerald City, our home. I smiled as I watched myself on my horse. My inner voice was guiding me today. It was as if I had fallen into the river and I was trusting the current to bring me to safety, I was going with the flow. We cling too much to the edges of rivers, for fear of the swift current. We all have to just let go and trust that all goes well.

"Diane, why are you talking to yourself?" asked Else.

"Oh, I'm just daydreaming out loud."

"What were you thinking of?"

"I was thinking of a story I read once." All of a sudden Gigglejuice and Sandy were leaning over the seat to listen, with Benny wide-eyed beside them.

"Okay, let's hear the story," said Gord as he tipped his hat.

"There was once an atheist."

"What's an atheist?" they all piped up.

"A person who doesn't believe in God," I answered. "Anyway, he was climbing a mountain. He slipped and fell over a cliff, but as he fell, he caught onto a branch. While he was hanging on for dear life, he called out, 'Is there anyone up there?' After a moment he heard a voice from heaven that said, 'I am here. I am God.' The atheist said, 'God, I know I have not been a believer, but if you rescue me and bring me to safety, I will forever serve you with respect and love.' God's voice said, 'My son, I love you and will look after you. All you have to do is trust me and believe in me. Let go of the branch.' The atheist thought for a moment. Then he yelled, 'IS THERE ANY-ONE ELSE UP THERE?'"

Everyone started to laugh, Gigglejuice louder than the others. Watching them laugh, I knew I had to trust the flow that I was now feeling. I felt wonderful, just letting go.

The bus pulled up at the company's favorite truck stop and everyone made a dash for the restaurant. I imagined that I'd tied Silver to a cactus and that he was waiting for me to return.

"I'm starving," Ted said to Benny.

Gord was way ahead of the group. "I got a table," he yelled. "Hurry, it's packed with people."

As usual, I headed to a pay phone to call Terry. She answered on the first ring.

"Famous People Players."

"Hi, we're at a truck stop, and the driver tells me we should hit our destination in about three hours. Everything is just great." I started to tell her about the tour. Suddenly she interrupted me.

"Have you read today's paper? It's front-page news."

"What is?"

"The Reichmann brothers are going under."

I was paralyzed.

"Are you still there?" Terry asked after a minute.

"I'm here. I can't believe I sent that fax to Pat last week, about how I wished I was with the Reichmann brothers. I'm in shock. I don't know what to say."

"Diane, the recession is awful. People are going bankrupt and getting laid off everywhere."

We talked for about a half-hour, with continual interruptions from Rossen telling me to come and eat.

"I ordered you a hamburger, Diane. Diane, the hamburger is ready. Come to the table, come before it gets too cold."

"Look, Terry, I gotta go, but give Pat a call. I'm worried about our arrangement with Mr. All-Talk and Mr. No-Action. Let's ease off a bit on the campaign. The Reichmanns' problems will make everyone in Canada scared to make a contribution."

As we boarded the bus, I grabbed my hamburger to eat as we drove on. I picked up *U.S.A. Today* and read the front page of the paper.

It's funny, I thought, how my inner voice had kept me in a faraway trance, going with the flow, not reading the news. It was as if it had the road map of my human journey and wanted to prepare me for the roadblocks that lay ahead. Little did I realize as I read the paper that the roadblock that lay ahead was the edge of a cliff. The whole bridge was blown out.

8
The Answer
Is You

When I got back from the tour, my welcome home felt like a door being slammed in my face. "We can't build the theater center. Everyone has bailed out," said Pat Anderson at our board of directors' meeting. "All the other groups who were supposed to lease the space from the developers have backed out or gone under."

Sitting there facing my volunteer board, a group of people who not only give a lot of their time, but help fundraise and contribute to the Famous People Players, I felt like a prisoner on death row who had run out of appeals.

"The recession did us in," said Charles Tisdall, chairman of the board, leaning forward on his cane. Charles, who had stood by me for years, was a distinguished silver-haired man in his late sixties.

"There is no home for the Famous People Players," said Judi Schwartz dejectedly. I could tell that she was thinking about the investments we had made on architects' fees, on the fancy brochures.

Where were we with no theater center? I wanted to cry. All the money we'd saved busting our asses on road trips, trying to promote something that was never going to happen, what was it all for? I felt like a complete failure.

"How are we going to face the players and tell them we've lost the money and our chance for a home? How can anyone face them?" I asked the board.

"It's the recession," said Ron Secker.

"Blame the recession, that's the easy way out," I said. "Well, I'm not going to blame the recession, I'm going to blame me. I should have waited to see if the developers were actually going to build before running up bills on fundraising firms, fancy brochures, and architects' fees."

"Diane, stop beating yourself up," Ron said. "Hindsight is a wonderful thing. If you had waited, you wouldn't have raised any money for the Famous People Players. You wouldn't have received the federal government grant. We would have been in much deeper trouble if the developers had gone ahead and you didn't have the money to pay them."

"We would have been sued if the theater had been built and we couldn't pay for it," said Pat.

I burst into tears.

"Can we sue the developers?" asked Gord Swayze.

"Sure, go ahead and sue," I said. "How do you get blood from a stone?"

"Assess the financial damages and let's figure out where to go from here," suggested Judi.

"All the money we have raised so far in the capital campaign is in a trust account, and we have a commitment from the federal government for $500,000. If we don't build our theater center, all the money has to be returned," I said.

"You're overreacting, Diane," said Ron. "People will understand that there is a recession on and that we have to restructure the dream and cut costs."

"These are the 1990s," Pat added. "This is a blessing in disguise."

"I quite agree," said Gord. "This is a blessing in disguise."

"Trust me, if the developers could have built on time, they would have," Pat said.

"How were you going to pay for upkeep with the economy so bad, let alone raise the extra money you're short for construction? The players don't tour like they used to." Charles looked at me sadly.

"I'm sure as I'm sitting here now," said Ron, "that Silver Mine would be thrilled to say that construction was going ahead. Nobody, I don't care who you are, wants money problems. If they had the money, trust me, they would be building the theater center."

I felt ashamed. The board was right. If the developers had had the money, they would be building. But all I could remember was that ground-breaking ceremony and that last-minute clause. It disturbed me deeply. I'd let the Famous People Players down, people who trusted me with their lives.

"I just don't know how on earth I can start all over again," I said. "We're broke, flat-busted broke. All the money from my speaking engagements is gone, and I can't even put my own two children through school."

Ron got up and came over to hug me. "Diane, there will be an answer for all this. You know as well as any of us, everything works out for the best."

"Time will tell," said Pat.

Charles stood up and said, "Meeting adjourned," as he came toward me to give me a hug.

When I talked to Terry, her news wasn't much better. "The box office is horrible," she said. "You don't want to know how bad. Tickets just aren't selling. Too many people out of a job. There will only be a small crowd of people at the next show."

"I'm tired of these ups and downs. I'm physically exhausted from picking myself up and starting all over again." I looked at her hopelessly.

"Thelma's gone," she said. "She had to get back to Texas. Her family needs her; she's been away from them too long."

"And I never said good-bye." I felt awful.

"She knows how busy you are. Don't worry about it. Honestly, she's fine. She wanted a quiet exit."

"I feel like the goose who lays the golden egg that never hatches," I said, picked up my bag, and trailed off to the theater to seek refuge in my dressing room.

With our capital campaign and the dream of our own home in ruins, we went to perform at the John Bassett Theatre in Toronto. My sciatic nerve was pumping so hard, I thought it was going to burst through my leg.

I was scared. It couldn't be the end of a dream, I kept thinking. How could it be? In spite of all the ingrates and the not-so-greats we had met on our journey down our yellow brick road, we had to reach our Emerald City, our home.

The players seemed different. They knew. I was sure that they knew we were in serious trouble. What opening speech could I give them? What words of inspiration could I say that would bring life back into a tired, discouraged group? I stared at my face in the dressing-room mirror, at the lines that carved the history of my life from the beginning of my dream when I first founded the Famous People Players.

"Oh God, Diane, you're thinking like an old woman in her nineties. You're only forty-four," I said to myself. "Get it together, Dupuy." But I couldn't get it together, I was too exhausted. I couldn't face the future, I could only dwell on the past.

Then I remembered the early days, when there was no audience. I remembered when Liberace first discovered us and took the Famous People Players to open for him in Las Vegas.

We loved hearing Lee's late-night stories after the midnight show. "You never know who is in the audience," he would say. His smile got bigger, and his eyes sparkled brighter than the rings on his fingers.

"Only eight people came to see my show," he told us once. "I was so upset. How could only eight people buy tickets to my performance? It was so embarrassing."

We knew the feeling.

"Me know," said Greg, one of the veterans of the troupe.

"I didn't want to perform. In fact, I flat-out refused. I was ready to cancel the show."

Everyone's eyes got big. Debbie Lim was listening intently as she sat cross-legged in front of the coffee table. She was feeling for the fruit, oysters, caviar, shrimp, and cheeses that had been put there for us to nibble on. Benny picked up an orange and placed it in her hands.

"What happened?" Debbie asked.

"I'll tell you what happened. I sat in front of my dressing-room mirror, and boy was I mad."

Everyone looked at each other. We could never picture Lee mad.

"You actually got mad?" I asked him.

"To tell you the truth, Dora," (he'd nicknamed me Dora Doom because I worried too much) "I was hurt. I wanted to cry. I wanted to perform so bad, and make people happy. Then suddenly it came to me." He reached over to pick a grape off a beautiful arrangement of fruit. "If those eight people thought enough of me to come out and see me perform, then I was going to give them the best damn performance they had ever seen. I went out on stage and knocked them dead. You know what? They loved me.

"After the show, I went to my dressing room. There was a knock at my door. When I opened it, there was one of the people from the audience. 'I just wanted to come backstage and tell you how wonderful you were,' the man said and he gave me his business card. He turned out to be a Hollywood manager called Seymour Heller who wanted to represent me, and that," he looked at all the Famous People Players, "is how I became a star. So remember, you never know who is in the audience."

"Are you okay?" Debbie Rossen pressed her head against my forehead, her eyes staring into mine. I suddenly came back to the present.

"I'm okay, Debbie. I was just thinking of Liberace. Trust me, I'm okay."

"Oh no, you're not. You've got to pull yourself together. We love you, Diane," she said, smiling.

"I love you too, Debbie."

"I know," she said, "but you worry too much. You're going to have a nervous breakdown."

She moved away and began organizing my junk that was littered all over the place.

"I can't get over how much you look like Bette Midler," I told her.

"Oh, you! Look, here are your glasses, you'll be looking for your glasses. How can you see without them? Here, put them on and see. When are we getting our home?"

I watched her hang up my coat and clothes as she kept talking away.

"Debbie, aren't you scared?" I asked her.

"Scared of what?"

"Well, the developers didn't build the building as they promised. There's a recession on and we have no money."

Debbie Rossen walked over to me and said sternly, "Pull yourself together. We love you. We're a family. We have each other. Here now, put your glasses on and you will see better."

Everything happens for a reason. Debbie came into my dressing room at this particular time, when I was thinking about Liberace, to deliver me a message. I just had to receive it. The message was the word "see."

"Debbie," I said, suddenly feeling stronger, "let's get the group together. We've got a show to do." New life came into me. I had energy, wonderful energy that I hadn't had since the capital campaign started. "It's all going to work out, I know it."

"Here she goes again," Rossen said to Lesley and Sandy as they entered the room.

"Oh no!" Lesley said, giggling away.

When everyone had gathered, I started to talk. "Today I have some bad news. We've lost our home. The developer can't build. Ron said to me today that everything happens for a reason and he is right. This property was not right for us. But we are going to build our home anyway. I don't care about the recession. For a while I forgot a very important lesson, and Rossen reminded me of that lesson. It was there all the time, right in front of me. The answer is you. All of you. You're the home. We are a family, just like Rossen said. This is *our* dream. It doesn't belong to anyone else but us. We will find the dream together and we will show all of them that *we* are the dream-makers."

"Diane," Benny said, "the audience is bad. Not many people out there tonight."

"Who cares?" I said. "What did Liberace say?"

"YOU NEVER KNOW WHO IS IN THE AUDIENCE!" everyone yelled in unison.

Quickly the performers took their places on stage. Phil Chart, our stage manager, was dancing in the wings to the pre-show music.

"House to half," he said. "Stand by, curtain and sound," he said into his headset for all the crew to hear.

"We've got a show to do. Break a leg!" He waved to the group who were pulling their hoods down over their faces. "And GO!" Phil gave the final cue as if he were at the races. The gates swung open and out came the horses. Actually, it was the curtain that went up and the magic of the Famous People Players that filled the stage.

Our dream was painted before my eyes. I had to go back to the Famous People Players to find the answer. Forget what the critics have to say about what works or doesn't work. What I believe, what the players believe, is what will work. Never again will I let someone tell me differently.

I realized that the people I'd been dealing with were people who didn't dream, people who didn't believe in magic, who'd forgotten what they once had as children. The miracle of life, the power of the soul. Children accomplish amazing things in a short period of time. They can even learn two languages. They are not afraid. They are comfortable with themselves, and their bodies. But as they grow and become adults, they lose this wonderful naïvety. They develop their minds at the expense of their souls. They put the inner child to bed forever and stifle the wonderful joy they once knew.

The Famous People Players perform on stage with humor and love, which comes naturally to them because they never put their inner child to bed. It's awake and alive in them all the time.

With this new energy and belief in ourselves we started all over again to look for a new home. We were not going to give up.

"God grant me the serenity to accept the things I cannot change, the courage to change the things I can, and the wisdom to know the difference," I said to myself.

One thing I've learned from Ron and the players is never to blame anyone for the situation, the disappointments, or the setbacks you experience. Don't make excuses about why something isn't happening. Although some people find this difficult to accept, everything happens for a reason.

The financial woes caused by the recession, the "kerfuffles" at Smoke and Mirrors, the development that didn't happen: these things came into our lives for a reason. They were an important ingredient in the growth of the Famous People Players. They taught us a lot about the business we were in. They showed us that we were survivors and that we would prosper if we followed our hearts and listened to our gut instincts. Never give up. Go forward with no regrets. Without those experiences we would never have learned anything.

We knew more about our dream and our company than any expert. After all, Famous People Players wasn't conceived by an expert. It was born from love and the will to dream. It was one thing for the experts to say that we needed to do this or that, but they were not the ones who were going to live with the results, let alone pay for them. I thought of Mark Twain saying "an expert was a guy from out of town." We were the experts and we knew what was best for us. It was time for me to put on my white hat and take that ride to find our home.

Every day we looked for a place to build our home.

"This is a great time to buy," I thought. Everything seemed to be available in recessionary Toronto. Warehouse after warehouse remained empty. People were practically giving things away. But there was always something wrong with each property we looked at. The taxes were too high or the location was wrong, there was no loading dock or there were too many pillars. The list went on and on.

"There is a gem of a property up for lease," a real-estate agent told us in 1992. "Long-term lease, which would be perfect. It's been empty for a long time, and it's in the right location."

Ron, Mary, Judi, and I drove over to take a look at the building near the harborfront. It was wonderful.

"The cost of renovations would be the same as the other development," said Michael Mitterhuber, our architect.

"Let's not get too excited. I'd hate to have another fall," I said to the real-estate agent.

But each time we went to see the property, with Ron and our contact from the federal government, our hopes got higher and higher.

"There are a lot of formalities to go through for this property," Dan said. "Zoning for one. This area is zoned for residential use only. Amendments to the zoning by-law would have to be made. For another thing, there's a condo above the space. The tenants are living in a residential building. They don't want to have the general public coming in and lots of noise. They pay for peace and quiet. The idea of a theater company might turn them right off. I don't know what they'll say when they find out that they're dealing with the handicapped."

I cringed when I heard that. But there was nothing I could do. I knew in my heart that if it was meant to be, it would be.

I called Ivan Fleischmann to come to our rescue. I wanted him to make sure the offer and the documents reflected our dream positively. Ivan worked hard to get the city onside and to find out how we could fit in with the zoning by-laws. The faces had changed at City Hall. Our friend Art Eggleton was no longer the mayor of Toronto. We had to start all over again.

Once again I felt as if I was riding a roller-coaster ride backward. City Hall is like that.

"Do I have to go to another meeting?" I pleaded.

"No one can tell your mission, your story better than you," Ivan said, as he dragged me along.

"Why do I feel like I'm going to the dentist's office for a root canal?" I asked.

In the end, after all Ivan's work, the National Ballet of Canada got the space. We didn't shed a tear. It was not meant for us after all. Their loss.

"Adrienne Clarkson called," said Terry as she interrupted a rehearsal. Adrienne Clarkson is one of Canada's finest interviewers, and the former representative of the province of Ontario in Paris. She has her own show on the CBC called "Adrienne Clarkson Presents."

I had made a submission to the CBC, suggesting that they do a one-hour special on the Famous People Players, and Adrienne had been approached by the head of variety programming to carry it on her show.

The special was to focus on the Famous People Players' need to raise money for their home, and would feature a fundraising gala in Ottawa with the prime minister of Canada.

This was 1992 and Canada was in the middle of a constitutional crisis. Trying to keep Canada together was the main objective for all politicians in the federal government, especially Joe Clark, minister for Canadian unity. The money that was being spent to hold the country together was well into the millions.

We decided to put together a show that would go right to the heart and soul of Canada. The first number would open with a powerful new arrangement of "O Canada" that had been recorded by major Canadian artists. Adrienne Clarkson and the CBC cameras were on hand for our first rehearsal.

When we create a new production, we don't have all the new and wonderful props and puppets that Mary creates. We had to use our bodies to bring the maple leaf, the beaver, the Canada goose, and the moose to life on stage. We got quite emotional rehearsing the number. The cameras followed us as we moved to the rhythm of the music. Debbie Lim pretended she was holding onto the maple leaf. Mary would design the maple leaf to slip onto her hand, with a mouth pocket for the maple leaf to sing the words to "O Canada." The beaver was one of my staff performers, Keith Albertson. The Canada goose flying across the stage was Benny. The moose was three people: Ted, Gord, and Debbie Rossen.

The Indian headdress was very special—the feathers would burst apart and turn into birds flying through the air. This magic moment needed eight people: Lesley, Michelle, Else, Sandra, and Darlene, as well as my daughters, Jeanine and Joanne, who were now working as staff. This would be followed by a tribute to Quebec with the fleur-de-lys. Then we had Canadian astronauts floating in space with the Canadian flag. At that point, the lights would show Adrienne Clarkson holding the Canadian flag. What an opening it was going to be!

The rest of the show was just as exciting. Each number featured a different region of Canada, from the east coast to the west. We began with a humorous number called "Bud the Spud." A giant potato would dance across the stage singing Stompin' Tom Connors' hit about the best potatoes from Prince Edward Island. Even k.d lang would come to life in black light, dancing to a barn-dance version of "Turn Me Around Polka."

As we rehearsed with our bodies, we looked absolutely ridiculous. Ted and Gord pretended they were a moose, Benny was a goose, and everyone else was feathers, potatoes, astronauts, or fleur-de-lys. The cameras followed each one of us as we improvised with the music, and our imaginations.

Mary, Therese, and Enrico were creating the actual props that would replace our imagination and float through the air, defying gravity.

"We need a really good ending," Jeanine kept telling me, but I couldn't think of one.

"Something will come to me when I least expect it," I told her.

People in Ottawa were excited about our arrival. We were particularly glad to see Barry and Anne McDougall. For years, this delightful couple had worked hard as volunteers to raise money for the Famous People Players. They were responsible for overseeing a committee of loyal friends who were out selling tickets to fill up the theater.

Anne is a tall, strong woman, with a wonderfully kind heart. I remember when I was selling T-shirts in the lobby of some theater, Anne came up to me at intermission and slipped me a $100 donation to the company. She did it very discreetly, she didn't want anyone to see.

ABOVE: Debbie Rossen
(left) and Michelle Busby
on opening night.

RIGHT: Jason Morgan
(standing, far right) instructs
the players on the finer
points of serving.

Diane's mother, Mary Thornton, and Else Buck, recipient of the Ron Secker Award for her outstanding work with the other members of the company.

Lloyd Bridges and the cast of the Famous People Players.

Diane's daughter Joanne *(left)* and Ginny Young.

Don Harron, a fine actor and writer and a great supporter of the Famous People Players, with Debbie Lim.

Tom Cruise and an inquisitive friend.

Robby Benson, chairman of the U.S. board and the voice of the Beast in Disney's *Beauty and the Beast*, shares a laugh with Diane Dupuy.

William Shatner hugs a delighted *Star Trek* fan, Darlene Arsenault.

Diane and her daughter Jeanine show off the Famous Peoples Players' Broadway billboard on Schubert Alley.

The Famous People Players introduce themselves to Phil Collins.

Phil Collins and the prop department (*left to right*: Enrico Basco, Sandra Wheatle, Phil Collins, Helen Lee, Therese Picco, and Mary Thornton).

The "other" Phil Collins.

Benny D'Onofrio and Annie Callingham, Phil Collins' assistant and a tireless friend of the Famous People Players.

Ted Billinger
Gord

Iris Billinger with her three sons, Gord *(left)*, Doug *(middle)*, and Ted *(right)*, and her well-deserved plaque for Parent of the Year.

Memory Lane, before and after.

Mary Thornton, Diane's mother, and Gord Swayze, director of the Famous People Players, raise their glasses in a toast.

Diane Dupuy and Governor General Ray Hnatyshyn at the ribbon-cutting ceremony.

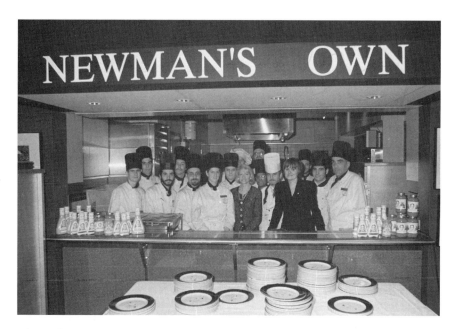

The staff with Ursula Hotchner (*center*), vice-president of Paul Newman's company, look out from their new kitchen.

Diane's husband, Bernard, and Wally, a volunteer, pour Annie Callingham a well-deserved drink.

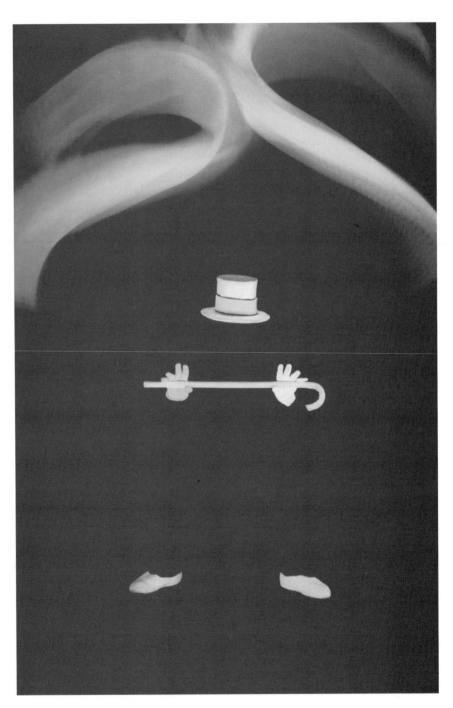

Our company logo—the invisible man.

But humble and quiet as she appears, don't ever say "Who are the Famous People Players?" to her. She'll deafen you. "What do you mean you have never heard of the Famous People Players?" Anne will yell at anyone who asks about us. "Where have you been living, under a rock?"

I always got a big kick out of her Monday-morning phone calls to me in Toronto.

"Well, I told them who you are," she'd say. "They now have enough material to write a book about the Famous People Players."

"We're going to break the party line," she told me when I got to Ottawa. "Mrs. Harvie Andre, wife of the cabinet minister, has done a wonderful job of getting all the house leaders from each party to sit on the committee. We're working together. Everyone responded with great enthusiasm." The committee's goal was to raise $75,000 to underwrite the prop shop, which they called the "Magic Room," for our new theater center. They were well on their way to achieving that goal.

Everything was going smoothly, except for the fact that we still didn't have a place to call home. I was afraid to tell Anne McDougall and our sponsors that the development was off for fear the fund-raising would screech to a permanent halt. So with anxiety in my heart, I continued to raise funds for the project.

"It's not completely off," Pat kept reminding me, "but it's not hopeful either."

"Let's see where we go," I said. "I've got to remember the river. Let's go with the flow, and pray it leads us to safety."

9

"This Place Feels Like Home"

Rehearsals were going great. The props made by Mary, Therese, and Enrico looked beautiful. In between rehearsals for the Ottawa production we made a short tour of the east coast of Canada. It was there that Benny picked up a copy of *Spy* magazine that had a wonderful article about the pop star Phil Collins.

"We should get him to see our show," said Phil Chart, puffing on a cigarette that I wished would be his last.

Famous People Players had been using a puppet of the famous star for a year by then, but we'd never got around to writing to him to let him know that we were bringing him to life on stage.

When I got back to Toronto, I wrote a letter to Phil Collins and enclosed a picture of his puppet and a copy of my book *Dare To Dream*. I also invited him to Ottawa for the opening gala. We wanted to honor him with a special award for the work he has done for so many charities, particularly the homeless. On his last tour he had donated a substantial amount of money to the food bank in Toronto.

It wasn't long before we got a wonderful response from his personal secretary, Annie Callingham. She called from England to let us know that Phil was touring in Australia. She said she knew how important our letter was and she would forward it to Phil.

We missed not having Liberace in our lives and I was hoping that Phil Collins could fill the void. Liberace had meant a lot to us personally and was an important part of the company's history. In *Dare To Dream*, which is a tribute to him, I described how Liberace first discovered the Famous People Players. When I say "discovered," I am really talking about my plot to hijack one of the greatest entertainers in the world. We wanted him to see us perform, and hoped that he would put us in his show in Las Vegas. I did everything from phoning his manager, Seymour Heller, pretending I was calling from the prime minister's office, to threatening to lie down in front of his limousine. This story was made into a CBS movie of the week called *Special People*, in which the American actress Brooke Adams played me (Liberace, naturally, played himself).

When Phil Collins read my book, he said, "Annie, let's do it the easy way. Let's say yes."

Phil couldn't come to Ottawa because of his touring schedule, but he promised to visit us in Toronto. Annie would represent him in Ottawa for the premiere of the new show.

"We'll go for dinner when Phil Collins' secretary comes to Toronto," Ron said, "and talk things over before we leave for Ottawa."

There were all kinds of last-minute changes to attend to. Phil Chart reminded me about the tapes that Ron had to record.

"I don't know what I'd do without Ron. He has been recording our show free of charge since the day I founded the Famous People Players," I said to Phil.

"He's the most patient person I've ever met," Phil said as he handed me a bag full of CDs with editing notes to give to Ron.

Phil Collins' tour brought him to Toronto to appear at the SkyDome with Genesis. Annie called from England to let us know we had free tickets.

"Phil Collins gave us tickets to his show," screamed Ted and Gord as they ran into the rehearsal hall. Everyone was thrilled.

"We'd better make his puppet look great," Keith told everyone.

Annie flew in from England to spend a week with the Famous People Players before the Ottawa gala. Her flight was due in from London around six in the evening. Terry and I went to meet her at the airport. Both of us were very nervous—we felt it would be like meeting Phil himself.

"If she doesn't like us," I said to Terry on the way to the airport, "I'll die."

I don't know what I was expecting. I thought she might be very glamorous and high-powered. Her husband was the talented Geoffrey Callingham, an engineer who had worked on all Phil's albums. One hears so many stories about the people who surround famous stars. I was trying to prepare myself for a gorgeous groupie of some sort.

"I'll park the car," Terry said. "You go meet her."

"No, I'll park and you meet her."

"No," she said firmly, "I'll park the car."

"No, I'll park it." We circled the airport five times, arguing over who would park the car. Finally we decided that we'd both park the car, and both of us would meet Annie.

As we waited for her flight to come in, a few people approached me, as I was wearing my Famous People Players T-shirt.

"You're Diane Dupuy, aren't you? I love your company, they are the greatest. Can I have your autograph?"

When I'd finished signing, I was approached by a woman with long straight hair, wearing a hat. "You're Diane?" she asked, in a strong English accent. "I'm Annie, and I'm tired."

She hugged me. Annie turned out to be one of the most down-to-earth people I've ever met.

"Now," she said, as she got into our company van, "I want to sleep. Tomorrow I'll get to work."

"Get to work?" I thought. "What does she mean?"

She answered the question in my mind. "I volunteer a lot in England and I'm not here to waste any time. I'm here to help you. So give me something to do."

Terry and I were amazed. We couldn't imagine Phil Collins' secretary working for us. We dropped her off at Mary's apartment.

"Don't worry, I don't smoke," Annie said to Mary, and went to bed.

I went home to rest for the big day tomorrow. But as soon as I opened the door, I found the house in an uproar.

"Leave my stuff alone," screamed Jeanine to Joanne. "You took my clothes. I want my sweater and tights back."

"You've got my lipstick," Joanne screamed back even louder. The bedroom doors upstairs slammed.

"Stop it, you two." I ran up the stairs.

"You stop it," said Jeanine. "She has my clothes."

"Give her back her clothes."

"Not until I get my lipstick back," said Joanne.

"Where's dinner?" Bernard had just come home from work. "I'm starved."

I ran back downstairs. "I'm tired, couldn't you make dinner for a change?"

"Come on, I worked all day."

"What do you think I did, nothing?"

I went into the kitchen. It was a mess. Dishes from last night were still in the sink.

"Jeanine, Joanne, you get down here right now." I could hear them fighting all the way down the stairs toward the kitchen.

"Look at these dishes! Now you girls get busy and start cleaning up," I yelled at them. I opened the fridge, took out a frozen chicken, and threw it into the microwave.

"Everybody pitch in." I was slamming cupboard doors.

"Stop!" Bernard said, "We'll send out for a pizza."

"Great idea." The girls were finally in agreement about something.

"Fine with me," I huffed. "I'm going to take a bath, and get away from all of you."

Sinking down into a hot tub full of bubbles, I started to think about how difficult it was to raise a family, to be a wife, mother, and friend to everyone, not to mention working together with the two girls. I needed a cleaning lady and a cook. I needed a wife to come home to. Giving the money from my speaking engagements to Famous People Players certainly took away those privileges for me and my family.

I played with my toe in the faucet. Bang, the bathroom door flew open. "And another thing," yelled Jeanine at me, "all you do is think of your company. The Famous People Players come first. Joanne and I have always taken a back seat."

"Jeanine, I'm not dealing with this now. I'm taking a bath. This is my private time. We will talk after you calm down."

"Calm down? How can I calm down? My sweater is missing, Joanne's wearing my shoes, and you expect me to rehearse at seven in the morning."

"I don't want to hear about it now. I want to be left alone."

Slam went the bathroom door. I sat there in the water feeling cold and empty. The bubbles had disappeared. I reached for the faucet and turned on the hot water to warm up the bath. As the water got nice and hot again, I realized how right Jeanine was. The children had taken a back seat to my dream. How could I change, how could I let them both know that I loved them very much and that they meant more to me than the Famous People Players? What was I doing wrong?

I'd tried to give them lots of compliments, especially when Jeanine took the time to help Sandra with her hygiene problems, and when she showed the patience that was required to teach the players their parts in the show. Joanne, too, had given so much of herself to the company. She performed alongside them, helping them to remember their parts in the show. She even took Lesley and the girls shopping at Victoria's Secret every time we toured in the United States. My two children were in many ways my sidekicks as I explored and looked for adventures. I couldn't have run the Famous People Players without them.

I was being too selfish, my heart was telling me. Jeanine and Joanne have their own dreams to pursue and I should encourage them to explore their own paths, whether they lay with the Famous People Players or not. I watched the water from the bath run down the drain. I dried myself off and went to bed early, no pizza for me.

❉

The next morning the players hurried into the rehearsal hall to prepare a private show for Annie. Everyone was running around, banging into each other as they preset their props.

"Quick," Joanne said, "get Phil's drums. Rossen, we need his drumsticks."

The adrenaline level was high. If the lights had burned out there would have been enough electricity from the performers to keep the black lights burning.

"Into your jumpsuits, now!" hollered Jeanine.

Mary's van pulled up and Benny raced into the rehearsal hall to tell us, "They're here! Let's not blow it!"

Annie came into the room, looking rested and said, "Well, let's get this show on the road. I've been dying to meet you all and see the Famous People Players. I've read so much about you."

The players went up to Annie one by one to introduce themselves.

"Hi. I'm Debbie Rossen."

"I'm Gord. This is my brother Ted. No, we're not twins."

I smiled as each one proudly carried on a conversation with Annie.

"Where's Phil? Did he come with you?" asked Ted.

"No," Annie chuckled, "he's on tour, but I promise you he'll come. You'll have to make do with me instead."

"We'll take good care of you for Phil," said Gord.

"Diane is always freaked out," said Darlene.

"You have to ignore her," said Charleen Clarke.

"She also cries a lot when we perform," said Debbie Lim.

"Say hi to Phil for me and tell him Darlene sends her best."

"Me too," said Rossen.

The house lights went down and the black lights came on. The players took their positions. Annie sat slightly off to the side because we had a pillar smack dab in the middle of our rehearsal stage.

The music began and the props burst through the dark. Watching Annie watch the show was so much fun. She loved everything she saw. Then the Phil Collins puppet appeared and sang Phil's hit, "You

Can't Hurry Love." Annie was in stitches watching her boss dancing on his drums.

"It's brilliant," she said, "just brilliant. He'll love it. Put more hair on his head, he's not that bald. Mind you, he's not that thin either."

This was the beginning of a wonderful week with Annie. She watched our rehearsals, spent time with the players, and became another mother to each of us.

That night we took Annie out for dinner. Ron was supposed to meet us at seven o'clock sharp, but he didn't show up. We waited for a long time before we ordered food.

"This isn't like Ron," I said to Annie and Terry. "Something must have delayed him. However, when you meet him, you'll see he's a real charmer."

An hour later, Ron showed up. He was in a miserable mood, he couldn't even smile.

"Is something wrong?" I asked.

"No, nothing. I'm just tired, that's all. It's been a rough day at work."

But we could all see that something was bothering him.

"I'll find out tomorrow," I thought to myself.

The next day was the day of the concert. Annie called us from a pay phone downtown. "Your tickets are waiting for you at the SkyDome. I'm on my way to meet Phil before the show. See you at the concert."

Seeing the company's idol perform live on stage reminded me of the first time Liberace had invited the Famous People Players to see his show at the O'Keefe Centre in Toronto. I had a sudden sense of déjà vu.

The performers showed up early and excited. They dashed toward the front-row-center seats. They were blown away by the size of the stage and the magnificent set.

Annie came rushing over with programs to give to each of the players. "Phil has autographed a picture of himself for each member of the Famous People Players," she said. She noticed that we had a camera with us. "You're not supposed to have cameras in here. If security sees it, they'll take it away and you won't get it back. I'll let you take a couple of pictures of Phil, but after that, hide the camera," said Annie.

The lights went down and the music roared in our ears. The audience of 75,000 started to scream. On came the famous rock-and-roll band Genesis, and there was our Phil.

What a night it was! Jeanine and Joanne had all the Famous People Players dancing with each other in the aisles. When Phil began to sing, the players nearly went crazy. It was worth every second of our rehearsals to make our Phil look like the one performing in front of us that night. If you've ever heard the song, "Love Makes the World Go Round," you'll know how we felt. All 75,000 people in the audience were loving Genesis and Phil, and Phil was loving the audience. When the concert ended we floated out on a wonderful high from such an extraordinary experience.

As Bernard drove members of the Famous People Players home, Jeanine, Joanne and I went home on our own to get ready for the big day tomorrow morning when Phil was to visit the Famous People Players and meet his puppet.

"He'll only have time to see his puppet, not the whole show," said Annie, calling from the Four Seasons Hotel. "He's very tired. He didn't get to bed until very late and he mustn't miss his flight."

The CBC camera crew arrived to prepare for the meeting of Phil with Phil. It would make a great moment in our television special.

I stood waiting for him to pull up to the front door. The performers were in the rehearsal hall. My mouth was dry. My hands kept shaking. Butterflies filled my entire body. Mary, however, was perfectly calm. She couldn't wait to tell Phil that the sound had been too loud last night at his concert.

"Much too loud," she insisted. "My ears are still ringing. All those people screaming. They should all sit quietly and listen to the music. No jumping up and down and making a spectacle of themselves."

"Oh, no," said Benny, "Mary is going to tell Phil off."

"Just keep her away from him. Don't let her meet him," I had told the players. Mary is seventy-nine, and this was her first rock concert.

Obviously it was an experience she would never forget. It was also likely to be one I would never forget if she told Phil Collins off.

We were watching for a limo, so we were surprised when a Jaguar arrived at the door. Out got Annie, her husband, Geoffrey, the drummer from the band, and then Phil.

He was clearly tired as he climbed the rickety old stairway of our warehouse. I was nervously doing most of the talking.

"I loved your show last night. You were great. I'm so glad you could come, it means so much to all the players. They adore you, and are so excited that you're here. They're nervous," I said, stumbling over my words. "Look who's talking," I thought.

I opened the doors to the prop-shop area, which is filled with a menagerie of props. The camera zeroed in on Phil's face, which must have been annoying for him. I led him into the rehearsal hall.

Leave it to the Famous People Players to break the ice. They broke into thunderous applause and introduced themselves with great pride.

"I'm Ted. This is my brother Gord. We're not twins." Annie and I smiled at each other.

"I'm Debbie Lim. Your concert was a blast."

"I'm Benny, you're the best. I like that bald-headed guy in your show."

Phil smiled.

Lesley, giggling away, shook Phil's hand. Then she said, "This is Sandra."

"Me Sandra." she looked down.

"I'm Debbie Rossen. Will you autograph my souvenir book for me?"

"You were all at the concert?" Phil asked them.

"YES!" they shouted. "It was great! Now come and see us perform, Phil."

We sat him down on one of our old chairs, hoping he wouldn't fall through the threadbare seat. I turned to Phil Chart and gave him the sign to bring down the lights and hit the sound.

Phil Collins leaned forward intently, his chin propped on his hand, and the music began.

You have no idea what it feels like to be sitting next to the person whose puppet is performing on stage. It's a terrifying experience. I imagined every single thing that could go wrong in the dark. What if the puppet of Phil came out and his head fell off his body? Or worse, what if his pants fell down when he jumped up and down in the skipping-rope scene?

Phil the puppet appeared, rolling his bass drum across the stage with his feet. He jumped off it and fluorescent green skipping-ropes appeared. Thank God his pants didn't fall down when he started jumping. On came a long set of floating piano keys, which he played with his feet. Drums of different sizes came on and formed a complete drum set, which he started playing.

The players wowed everyone when the drum set moved across the stage as Phil the puppet played. And no, his head didn't roll off his body. At the end, all the people in the audience, including the camera crew, were on their feet. The performers took their hoods off their sweating faces. Phil leapt from his seat and hugged each of the players. He wasn't tired anymore.

I burst into tears with the emotion of it all. I tried to express in words, in front of the cameras, how much this visit meant to us. I thanked Phil for the wonderful work he does for so many people. We gave him a plaque that said: "Thanks for having trust in us. Famous People Players." Phil gave me a big hug. The softness of his suede bomber jacket felt good.

It was wonderful watching Phil talk to all the players. The warmth that came from him was like a light that touched each of us. He called his puppet "Phil Junior" and the players were calling him "Uncle Phil."

"Diane has a dream for us," Ted told him.

"We want a home. A place where people can come and visit us," said Debbie Lim.

"It would have a restaurant," said Benny. "They could eat, we would cook the meals."

"Then they'd come and see a show," added Rossen.

"It's hard," said Gord, "but we're looking every day for a new home, Uncle Phil."

At that moment a drip fell from the ceiling onto one of the black boxes.

Annie came up to Phil. "Phil, you'll have to go, you're going to miss your plane."

"Oh no," everyone said, "we wish we could show you some more numbers."

Phil turned to Annie, "I want to see this."

He sat down again and the company moved quickly to perform our aquarium number and the top-hat-and-cane number, our company logo.

Annie looked worried. "Your flight. You'll be late."

Phil smiled and hugged everyone. Just as he was leaving, Mary came up to him.

"Oh no," I thought, "she's going to tell him his music was too loud." I shook as she went up to him.

"Phil, I'm Diane's mother, and I wanted to tell you how wonderful your concert was last night. I wouldn't have changed a thing. You were wonderful. Thank you for supporting the company. It means so much to us."

Phil gave her a big hug and thanked her.

"Next time you come," Benny said, "we'll have a new home, not this place."

Phil suddenly stopped to take a last look at the players. He looked around at all the puppets and props that hung from the ceilings and said, "This place feels like home to me."

We arrived in Ottawa to set up the stage for filming the show. We'd created puppets of the politicians that SCTV star Dave Thomas would interview. We'd portrayed the politicians, not as cartoon characters, but as what they stood for. Pierre Trudeau was a tall rose with a large thorn. Brian Mulroney was King Kong with a long chin. Jean Chrétien was a crab who spoke out of the side of his mouth. Audrey McLaughlin, then leader of the NDP, was a skinny bird beating a drum. Joe Clark was an octopus, because he had the job of keeping the country together.

"O Canada" brought the audience to its feet, and the puppets of the politicians had the politicians rolling in the aisles. "Bud the Spud," k.d. lang's polka, and Catherine McKinnon's "Farewell to Nova Scotia" had everyone clapping to the beat of the music. But the best part was the ending.

I'd finally come up with a great finish. It had come to me when I lost a major benefactor of the Famous People Players' Ottawa show, because he refused to be listed in the program with one of his competitors. Saddened by the loss of the donation, I'd got into my car to drive home to get away from it all. The radio was playing the Roy Orbison and k.d. lang duet version of "Crying." I cried through the whole song. When I arrived home, I called Terry to tell her I was coming right back.

"Don't let anyone go home. I've got one hell of an idea."

The Canadian and Quebec flags performed the duet. When the politicians saw this, they laughed at first, but then as the song went on they got very quiet. The Canadian flag sang how it was all right for awhile. Then the Quebec flag sang how I saw you last night... then stopped to say hello. As both flags finished with the lyrics about cryin' over you, I could see some of the politicians wiping away tears.

It was the biggest standing ovation in the history of the Famous People Players. The company took a bow, then I walked out on stage, stood before the cameras, and said, "I keep hearing from the press that this country needs to be saved, but I don't think that's the answer. What we need to do is reach inside our souls and believe in ourselves. Because when you believe in yourself everybody believes in you. Then wonderful things happen."

The next morning we met in the lobby of the hotel and organized ourselves for the long drive home. Everyone was exhausted. The players slept in their seats. Annie snuggled down between Ted and Gord at the back of the van, and Tom O'Donald and I took turns driving.

There was no conversation, just silence. By the time we hit Toronto, we were all starving. The parents had come to pick up the players, and Annie went back with Mary to her apartment.

"Mom, I want to talk to you," said Jeanine. Joanne was standing beside her.

"I'm sorry for what I said the other night. I didn't mean it, honest I didn't."

"Me too," said Joanne.

"I know you didn't." I hugged them both. "I think you girls are right and I'm wrong. It's hard being a parent." I looked at them both. "Daddy and I have an awful time of it sometimes. We've never been parents before. All we know about parenting is what our parents taught us. We take the good and bad from them and apply it to raising you two and you will do the same for your children. I give you lots of compliments but I don't give you enough space with me and Papa together as a family without the Famous People Players. We never take any vacations together, because work and touring always get in the way. I'm sorry."

"I'm sorry too, Mommy." Joanne looked up at me with her beautiful blue eyes. "We love you. I want to take over the company one day, I love it."

"I want to be a journalist," said Jeanine, "but that doesn't mean I don't love the company. I do. I love the people and I love helping people. That's what you've taught us, Mom."

"We'll work together and try not to let our family problems interfere with the company," I said.

"And try not to let the company interfere with our family," said Joanne.

We looked up and there stood my husband, Bernard, who is there for me all the time. "Look, Dupuy," he said, "you worry too much. Come on," he said to the girls, "we have to get home and have dinner."

"I'll follow you in my car," I said. "I should be home in an hour. I have a few things to do."

"Hurry up, Mom," said Jeanine.

"Yeah," said Joanne, "I'm leaving the phone off the hook, so we won't be disturbed as a family."

"Dad, let's have junk food tonight, let's pig out big time," said Jeanine. The door shut behind them.

I was left alone inside the rehearsal hall. The darkness engulfed me. The pipes groaned and a drip from the ceiling landed on my nose. Only a couple of days before, Phil Collins had walked through here. The cameras and the adrenaline of the performers had lit up the whole room, a room that "Uncle Phil" called home.

His words, "This place feels like home to me," kept pounding in my head. Maybe the grass isn't greener on the other side of the fence. Maybe we've been searching for a home, not realizing we've had a home all the time. I thought about the end of *The Wizard of Oz*, when Dorothy says to the Good Witch, "If I ever go looking for my heart's desire again, I won't look any further than my own backyard because if it isn't there, I never really lost it to begin with."

Riding my horse, Silver, down the yellow brick road showed me, like Dorothy, that I had to learn for myself. I'd been home all the time. All the dark angels I'd encountered were really blessings in disguise.

Was it possible to transform this dump into our dream? I walked around, a little afraid I'd meet a rat. I walked carefully down the rickety staircase that Phil Collins had climbed. The main floor on the other side was empty. It was waiting for someone to rent it and call it home. It was the perfect size for a restaurant. The tunnel leading from one building to the other was made of aluminum. I could hear the wind outside as I walked along it. We stored our costumes here. It was too narrow for an office. Could it be transformed into a gallery leading to the theater? And the theater, our rehearsal hall—it had all those pillars. How could it be transformed?

I started to dream as I walked through the building. I let myself float away and called on Liberace to be with me. I imagined the warehouse as a beautiful, well-designed building. The pillars came down, the carpet was laid, the walls were painted. I imagined Liberace helping me as I moved from room to room with him. I envisioned everything coming together so easily. It was right. Maybe we couldn't have a five hundred-seat theater as we'd planned. Maybe we weren't going to be across from the SkyDome, but for us the sky was still the limit.

The power inside me was strong, stronger than my imaginary Silver whose heart pounded hard, telling me to stop. Was it possible that all the people I'd met, who had tried to help, couldn't help because we weren't going in the right direction? It had taken Phil Collins to come and show us.

As I walked out of the rehearsal hall, I saw our company logo, the top hat and cane, at the front door. Someone had left it there by mistake. Had it been left there to let me know that this would be the main entrance to the theater?

I thought of what the great psychiatrist Victor Frankl had said to me when I visited him at his hospital bed in Vienna. "It's not what you expect from life, Diane, but what life expects from you. You, Diane, are a great doctor of the soul, a great logotherapist." (Logotherapy is a meaning-centered psychotherapy.)

The adrenaline flowed through my tired body, and I started to feel new life. Tomorrow I would call the architects and ask them if all this was possible.

Like Dorothy, I repeated over and over in my head, "There's no place like home, there's no place like home, there's no place like home."

I shut the door behind me.

10
Looking
at the Stars

Michael Mitterhuber, our architect, arrived early in the morning to take a look, for the first time, at the walls and the foundations of our old warehouse on Sudbury Street. "You must be kidding," he said. "Are you absolutely sure the other site is a no-go? This will be a big job."

Rossen stood close to me with her hands on her hips, looking up at Michael who is so much taller, "Oh you think so, eh? Well, our Uncle Phil said this feels like home and our Uncle Phil is right."

Michael smiled down at her and proceeded to explain the difficulties that we would encounter. Then he began to take notes and measurements so that he could draw up an estimate for the work.

"Well," Rossen said to Michael each time he wrote the measurements in his book.

When he was finished, he closed his notebook. "I won't know how much it will all cost for a couple of weeks."

"How come?" she asked.

"It takes time," he said.

"Oh you think so," she said, with her hands still on her hips.

A couple of weeks passed before Michael called me back.

"The most expensive thing will be the structural changes,

removing the pillars and installing air conditioning. And you'll need an elevator to take you to the theater. We estimate about $1 million to complete the project."

What a saving. This was fantastic news. It was just as Ron had said, "A blessing in disguise." I started to say so to Michael when he interrupted me.

"Wait, I'm not finished. Whether you want to hear this or not, there is one issue that has to be dealt with before you go any further, and that's zoning."

"Zoning!" I yelled, "I hate zoning! Not City Hall again."

"I'm afraid so. This area is not zoned for a theater. A rehearsal place, yes, or a place to build props, no problem. You can even have a restaurant, but no live performances."

I sank in my chair as Michael continued. "There's the fire department's approval, the building inspector, the planning commissioner ... the list goes on."

"Oh God, why can't I just do what I want to do?" I bit my lower lip. After a moment I hung up and called Ivan Fleischmann.

"Ivan, it's Dupuy. We're going back to City Hall again."

He started to laugh. When I'd explained to him in detail what we were doing, he took the positive approach. "We, Dupuy, are going to get the approvals. No one is going to stop you from building a home for the Famous People Players."

"Oh yeah? Well, why is it I can still feel the burn from the scrapes I've taken from our past visits to City Hall?"

"We're going to make this work," he insisted. "I think everybody at the city will do anything to make sure that you get your home."

At least the first step was easy. The landlord was more than enthusiastic, and our lease was extended to twenty years.

Selling the new location to the government was Judi's job. After a week she called me.

"Well, Diane, the good news is that the government does not want another feasibility study done. The bad news is that we have to reapply for funding."

"What!You mean to tell me that after all that work was done by those professional consultants—all those months and months—we have to apply all over again?"

"Calm down.We're lucky. It could have been worse.They could have asked for another feasibility study. This time I can do the work myself. I will put together the application and work with the government."

I needn't have worried. Judi was able to win over the government with her expertise and enthusiasm for the new site. "Just one more hurdle and it's a done deal," she told me. "We just need to get planning permission and then funds will be released."

So Ivan, with great energy, once again took on City Hall.

I sent a letter to all the people who had donated money to the capital campaign, to tell them we'd changed the location. It was not going to be a five-hundred-seat theater as we'd originally planned, but a wonderful one-hundred-seat theater, restaurant, and art gallery.The whole dream turned into an educational project that would benefit many people.

I went to see Ron to tell him how everything was unfolding.

"I was surprised at how everyone was relieved.They all prefer this site to the last one.Anne McDougall was thrilled.You and Pat were right. Everyone understood that we had to restructure the dream. Unfortunately, one benefactor, the one we'd hoped to name the theater after, declined.We lost a major corporation for funding. Still, I really think everything is for the best. Aren't you going to say anything? You're so quiet."

Ron was silent for a few minutes.Then he spoke. "Diane, the night I met you and Annie for dinner, I'd received some bad news."

"What, Ron? What happened?"

"I have cancer.The doctors think I've got less than six months." Tears filled his eyes.

"Ron!" I leapt from my chair. "Don't you dare give up! There are so many wonderful cures through diet."

"Diane, I don't think so."

"Oh yeah? Well you wait and see. The first thing we are going to do is go on a macrobiotic diet."

"*We* are going on a macrobiotic diet?" Ron smiled for the first time. "I'll do it with you. We'll work together."

As I hugged him I could sense his depression lifting slightly.

"Okay, where do we start?" he said.

"Tomorrow we'll go for lunch at the health store. We'll buy books on the subject and eat well. These doctors don't know what they're talking about," I said.

"Okay, Doctor Dupuy. I'll see you tomorrow, but don't keep me waiting."

I'd turned to leave when Ron said, "How are we going to make up for lost revenue from that dumb benefactor?"

"Getting better already, are we?" I said. "I know in my heart we made the right decision, Ron. Everything will work out. You'll see. That goes for you too."

Driving back to Famous People Players that afternoon, I kept thinking that I could cure Ron, and get myself healthy at the same time. "It's got to work, it's just got to," I said to myself over and over. "He's my wizard."

This time around planning the new home was fun. I ran from room to room, working with Michael on the layout and the interior design with Debbie Rossen always at my side.

"What do you envision here?" he would ask.

I looked around the barren room that had been added to the Famous People Players' newly signed lease. It was the space that would become the restaurant.

"I've always loved Art Deco, ever since we performed at Radio City Music Hall in New York. Make it look like that. And I want it to be warm. A feeling that there is a lot of love here, even when it's empty. The kitchen will show off the talents of the performers cooking the meals. It has to be as special as the Famous People Players themselves."

"Then you'll be happy, won't you, Diane?" said Debbie.

"Yes, Debbie, then I will be happy."

I continued planning with Michael. "I want this to be the main entrance. I also want it to reflect Paul Newman."

"Paul Newman?" Michael asked, startled.

"Oh you," said Debbie, "don't you know anything?"

Suddenly Gigglejuice appeared, laughing away. "What do you say when we tell you we know him?" she said.

I started to explain, when Ted and Gord showed up. "Oh no you don't, dearie," said Ted, "I'll tell him." He turned to Michael. "A long time ago when we were performing in New York, Paul came to see our show. It was a big surprise."

"Yeah, Diane almost peed her pants," said Gord.

"What would you say he was drinking a beer at the bar," Gigglejuice said, remembering.

"I can't tell you how wonderful he really is," I told Michael.

"He's one in a million," said Gord.

"He loved our show," continued Ted.

"He came backstage to see us, so there," said Rossen, with her hands on her hips. "He said, 'I have the easy job, I sign the checks.'"

Paul had made a huge contribution to Famous People Players. I explained to Michael, "He made a donation from the sales of Newman's Own products. Famous People Players became Paul's first contribution to a Canadian charity."

As desperate as I had been to receive his first contribution with his autograph on a check for U.S. $20,000, instead of using it to pay bills, I'd put it into a trust account for the building fund. Through the financial contributions from Newman's Own over the years, that trust account had kept building up.

Years later, we opened on Broadway. Paul brought his wife, Joanne Woodward, to see our show. This time when he came backstage, I had a beer waiting for him. As I told Michael the story, Gigglejuice's laugh got louder.

"When he snapped the lid, the foam of the beer went all over his suit," said Ted.

I could see the scene in my head. He'd just smiled that gorgeous smile of his.

"He liked our black books," said Ted.

"What are black books?" asked Michael.

"Because we can't read, we have pictures of our props so we don't forget how to set them up."

Michael looked puzzled. "Oh you," said Rossen. "The fish number will have a picture of a fish."

"I get it," he said.

The performers had looked so cute, they'd all lined up single file to meet Paul and Joanne and shown them their black books. I started to reminisce with Michael as the players looked on.

"I remember little Michelle that night. It's an inside joke here at Famous People Players—because she's so tiny, we call her the tallest member of the company. She was the first in line to show her black book to Paul and Joanne." Gigglejuice laughed and nodded in agreement.

"I perform a seaweed in the fish number, a musical note in the Liberace number, and all of these." She'd flipped open each page of her book, proudly showing off her parts to Paul and Joanne. "Did you like these when you saw them on stage?" she asked them.

"Joanne loved the show," said Gord.

"She's a real nice lady," said Ted.

"Tell Michael about Greg," said Rossen to me.

"Well, next came Greg. He had his black book too. 'Me do this, me do that, and me do this,' he said to them." The players joined Gigglejuice in a big laugh. "By the time Joanne and Paul went through the line, it must have been an hour later."

I remember that evening, sitting down on our black boxes on stage, talking to them. It was one of the most relaxing conversations I'd ever had with anyone.

"They made us feel real good," said Gord.

I'd told Paul, "I have the money that you have contributed to the Famous People Players invested safely in a trust fund for our building. I've always wanted to start up a wonderful restaurant, where the veterans of the company who no longer perform will graduate. There, they will learn to cook and serve and further enhance their life skills. I just want to know what you think of that idea."

Paul had stared at me intently with those beautiful blue eyes of his, and said, "Diane, that's a beautiful dream. I think you should go for it!"

"Thank God!" I said. "Because I want you to pay for it."

When I told Michael about this, everyone started to laugh louder than Gigglejuice herself.

"That's why I want this restaurant to be very special," I told Michael. "Paul trusted us with his money, but even more importantly, he trusted us with his name. The restaurant is going to be called Newman's Own."

In truth, I wanted to call it that not just because of Paul's financial support, but also because of his attitude. There's a wonderful postscript in his cookbook, which sums up many of the things I believe too: "What I like is when life wiggles its hips and throws me a surprise. All the experts said we couldn't produce these foods without chemical preservatives; they said we couldn't use fresh garlic and onions; they said we had to advertise; they said no business in the world could give away 100 percent of its profits. Well, we didn't listen to any of 'em and just look at us. I feel that spreading our products around is spreading the gospel, and I'll stay at it as long as I enjoy it—and, as of now, I'm having a fine time." Newman had clearly come to the same conclusion about experts as we had. He was the ideal person to name the restaurant after.

As Michael walked around taking notes, he asked, "Where do you want the kitchen to be? It can be here," he said, pointing at one area, "or over there."

"There, I think," I said.

All of a sudden Mary, my mother, was beside us. "No! You want it there!" she said, pointing to the other spot.

"No, I want it here," I insisted.

"You want it there. You'd have more space if it was there."

"Oh no! Here they go again. Always fighting," sighed Gord.

"Michael," Mary tugged at his sleeve, "tell her she's wrong."

"Look, it doesn't matter," Michael said. "You fight it out between the two of you and give me a call. I should have the preliminary drawings to you by the end of next week."

"Next week?" we yelled in unison. "Why not tomorrow?"

"Tomorrow? Impossible. A lot of thought has to go into this. Besides, we still haven't decided on where the kitchen is going to be." He smiled and said good-bye, leaving Mary and me having a big fight in the middle of the empty room with Ted, Gord, Debbie, and Gigglejuice standing around us, watching.

All day long Mary and I were at it over the kitchen issue. Then Michael called and said it would cost extra for the plumbing and the ventilation if the kitchen went where Mary wanted it. As far as I could see that settled the argument, but Mary still looked stubborn.

"There, are you happy now?" Rossen asked.

"Very happy," I replied smugly.

I met Ron for lunch at the health food store. He was already waiting when I arrived.

"I found this book on macrobiotic diets. It sounds wonderful. I can't wait to get started," he said.

After eating a delicious lunch at the health food bar, we both admitted we had more energy.

"I've got to get back," I said to Ron.

"You're always in a hurry," he said.

"I know, but I have to get back to work. There is so much to do. Let's stock up on groceries and we'll meet here for lunch every day, how's that?" I said.

"Wonderful. Then you can fill me in on all the activity at Famous People Players. Did you bring the CDs for me to record?"

"No. I thought Gord should. You know how much he likes to visit you."

"I think it's the new receptionist we have at the office," Ron said. "She's cute and he loves to tip his hat to her."

When the drawings were finished, Michael rolled them out on our wooden table. We were speechless with awe.

"Look at the dining room," said Benny. "Where do I stand? I'm the maître d'."

"No! I'm the maître d'," argued Ted.

"Stop it, you two! You're both the maître d's," I said, to settle the argument.

"The cloakroom is next to the open kitchen. The kitchen is designed so that people walking past can see what you are cooking before hanging up their coats," I explained.

"Oh, right," said Ted. "If they don't like the food we're making, they can leave."

"Knock it off, Ted," said Benny, "they'll see me cooking."

"I thought you were the maître d'," Debbie Lim reminded him.

"You can't be both," added Charleen. "That's not fair. I'll be in the kitchen, they'll see me," she said, with a smirk at Benny.

We walked up the staircase to the top of the aluminum tunnel connecting the buildings.

"The tunnel is going to be your picture gallery," Michael said, leaning against the wall to look at it.

"What I was thinking is that we'd frame and hang up all our reviews and all the pictures we have from our travels," I said. "A history of the Famous People Players. As the people walk through the tunnel, they'll get even more excited about seeing the company perform."

Michael kept taking notes of all my ideas as we toured each room.

"I get to hang them," said Charleen.

"Oh no you don't," said Lisa, "you're in the kitchen, remember? Me and Rossen will hang the pictures, so there!"

"Who's going to keep them clean?" asked Lesley.

I turned and looked at her and said, "You and Sandra."

We were just about to move on, when I stopped Michael. "Wait a minute. Let's go back to the staircase. Something bothers me." We turned around and went back through the aluminum tunnel and down the staircase. "It looks awful. What are we going to do with this?"

"All you can do is paint it, fix up the stairs, and add some better lighting. It will be fine," said Michael. "Remember, you're on a tight budget, and the money must be spent wisely."

"You're worried about this?" Rossen looked at me with curiosity.

"It's not right." I kept staring at the rickety stairway. "I'll think about it. Let's go on." I skipped every second step to get to the top. We walked through the tunnel and into the rehearsal hall to look at the pillars.

"This," Michael explained, "is the worst job of all. Taking the pillars out. They're holding up the entire building. This is what most of your money will be spent on. But in the end you'll be amazed at the difference. The room, which looks small now, is really quite large, and will comfortably hold 120 to 200 seats. It's up to you. The stage will be right where you have it now. That way you save money, by removing only a couple of pillars instead of all of them."

Before I could respond, Mary appeared and interrupted. "No, no, no!" she said. "Don't be ridiculous. The stage must be at the other end." She went back to the entrance of the tunnel, then turned around and explained. "The audience should be facing the stage as soon as they walk into the room. They shouldn't turn to the left as they come in, but walk right in. Then you have something. Remember," she added, "everything that's cheap is more expensive." She shuffled off in her ratty old slippers.

Michael answered, "If that's what you want, then you have to pay for it. All this is possible. It's just going to cost money."

We sat down in silence on our orange crates. A mouse scurried by.

"Let me sleep on this," I said. "Mary's right. If we're going to do this, let's do this right and not in a half-assed way. I've had enough asses to deal with in my lifetime. Tell me what the increase in the price would be and we'll decide then."

Everyone departed quickly. Mary returned to the prop shop to finish painting the giant octopus for the Beatles' Octopus Garden. The performers got ready to go home. Lockers were slamming shut, and Mary was yelling to Ted and Gord not to forget to take the garbage out.

"You." I looked up and there was Rossen beside me. "Here, I made you a tea," she said.

"Thanks, Deb." I took a sip.

"You're worried, aren't you?"

"I'm very worried, Debbie. We have only so much money, and everything is so expensive. I honestly don't know what I should do. The stage should be there, Mary is right."

"She still wants the kitchen moved," Debbie said with a sigh.

"Well, she can forget that. I can't believe she is still going on about that kitchen," I said, shaking my head.

Debbie started to follow me back through the dark tunnel. We could hear the wind blowing through it.

"Careful you don't trip over the boxes," I said to her.

"Diane, I don't have a mother. You're my mother, Diane."

"Oh, Debbie, we all love you here."

"I know, this is my family. I have no family, and no father, just my brother in Zurich and Mrs. P. who looks after me, and Duncan too. I love the company so much. I want to see this place finished and I want us to have a home."

"We do have a home. Remember what Phil Collins said? 'It feels like home to me.'" We both laughed as we came to the end of the tunnel, and stood at the top of that awful rickety staircase.

"What to do, what to do?" I carried on a conversation in my head.

"Wait till it's all done, Diane, and Uncle Phil comes back. He'll just die when he sees all this, won't he, Diane? He will, he will just die, maybe wet his pants too, eh Diane?"

"Yeah, Debbie, maybe that too."

"Where are you gonna get the money?" Debbie kept talking.

I looked at the walls, and I noticed a crack that had extended itself further across to the other side. "I don't know just yet."

We stood at the bottom of the staircase, looking up silently. Only the pipes could be heard in the distance.

"Debbie, someone once said, I think it was Oscar Wilde, 'We are all in the gutter, but some of us are looking at the stars.' How true, how very true."

We shut off the lights and went home.

"Judi, am I ever glad you came! Here are the drawings that Michael put together. I want you to follow it like a treasure map."

"Don't go so fast, slow down," she said. While she held the drawings, I gave her a guided tour of the building. "Here's the main entrance. These main doors will be etched glass, with Liberace's name and piano and candelabra on them. I want this for Lee to symbolize how he first opened the doors for us in our career. This is the main dining room. That's where the kitchen will be."

"Mary told me the kitchen is to be somewhere else."

"Oh no! Is she still on that kitchen kick?"

"I'm just telling you what she said."

"Forget it!" I kept going. "Then, after people eat their dinner, which the company will prepare———"

"Wait a minute! Who's going to do the cooking?"

"Well, er, Mary. I haven't told her yet."

"Diane, think! Mary builds props, she can't cook and build props at the same time."

"Don't worry, I'll figure it out later. Keep moving." We walked on. "The staircase . . . ignore it, I haven't figured it out yet, but I will. You know, yesterday, it was so funny. Rossen and I were standing right here at the bottom looking up, when I thought of Oscar Wilde. 'We are all in the gutter, but some of us are looking at the stars.'"

Judi laughed. "You should put that phrase on this door."

We were walking up the two flights of stairs when it hit me. "STOP THE PRESSES!" I said, as I ran back down the stairs, leaving Judi leaning over the railing looking down at me. "That's it, Schwartz! I've got it!"

"What have you got, Dupuy?" She looked puzzled.

I raced back up the stairs to face her. "Remember how I told you everything is going over budget? We need more money."

"Yes."

"Well, this is it. The Stairway to the Stars! We'll sell stars with people's names on them, to help pay for the building cost. It will wake up this awful staircase and make it look sensational! Fluorescent stars! Small ones, medium ones, and big ones. The bigger the star, the more money. This, Judi, will be the most important room in the building. I love it. I just love it!" I was yelling at the top of my lungs as I ran up the stairway, through the tunnel and the rehearsal hall and into the prop shop.

"Judi?" I turned around. "Where are you?"

"Hold on, slow down." She came through the prop-room door.

"That's going to be the backstage door."

"Great! Now, where's a chair? I'm pooped." I found a chair for her to sit on.

"We're going to sell stars. Everybody wants to be a star. We'll sell lots and lots of stars."

"Diane, you know how I always cringe when I hear the word 'we.' What do you mean by 'we'?" She had that look in her eyes that said, "If you ask me to sell stars, I'll bop you one."

"Don't worry. You won't have to sell stars. Just get the money out of the government."

"That I can do. That I will do. Just give me a budget that doesn't keep changing on the construction site. How much are we short, exactly?"

"I won't be sure until Michael gives me a new budget, but I guess $100,000."

"Great. $100,000. How much are the stars going to sell for? Wait, let me guess. $100 for the small ones, $250 for the medium-sized ones, and $500 for the large, right?"

"Corporations will have to pay $1,000 per star. I only have to sell a hundred. I'll start tomorrow."

11
Saying
Good-Bye

The star campaign got off to a roaring start. I was selling stars left, right, and center. All kinds of people wanted to have their name on a star. Parents of the performers bought stars for their families. I just needed someone to pay for the staircase and have their name on it for a huge sum of money. That way I wouldn't have to worry about the construction cost and the special lighting needed for this area.

The fax machine became my best friend and my worst enemy at the same time. Each peep brought me good news or bad news. The good news, a star was sold. "Please order me one large star in bright yellow. Send me an invoice for $1,000. Make sure it's in a great location." The bad news always came from the architects' firm. "We have to replace the air conditioning. It will cost $250,000. This does not include the taxes. Have a good day," Michael faxed.

I called him back. "$250,000! This is too much! We're not the f—ing SkyDome!"

"It's not my fault," Michael explained. "You said, do it right or don't do it at all. It's an old building, Diane. That Mickey Mouse system that cost $15,000 wasn't going to cool 10 people, let alone 150 people. The engineer's report said——"

"I don't give a damn what the engineers said! Get it cheaper!" I kept yelling into the phone. "Michael, you don't understand. We're not some fat-cat corporation where you present a budget, and when it increases everybody nods their heads and runs to the well. There are no people nodding their heads here. In fact, I'm ripping my hair out. As for that well, if you tell me where it is, I'll go to it. As it stands, there is no well."

I admit I'm not the easiest person to work with when it comes to the completion of a dream. But I was physically tired from fundraising, and the money was being spent as fast as it came in. I was scared.

Each day I met Ron at the health food store. After eating there we always felt so energetic that we could have cartwheeled out of the store.

"I'm feeling terrific," said Ron. "My doctor said my cancer has shrunk, so I don't have to go for chemotherapy."

"Great news, Ron," I said. "I knew we could lick this."

I gave him the latest news every day. "We've hired the contractor that Michael recommended," I told him. "He's a nice man named Brent Hayman. Young, Ron, I mean really young. I think he is in his twenties. You'd like him, he's got a great heart and he's very patient."

"Boy, you need someone like that to work with you," said Ron, laughing.

"He's committed to realizing the dream. You know better than anyone, Ron, that it takes special people to work with special people, and Brent is truly special. He's making sure that all the construction workers that are hired have the company's best interest at heart. Mary is looking forward to making him spaghetti to carry him through the afternoon."

"And let me guess, Benny is assistant to Brent," Ron interrupted me.

"Right on," I said. "Everyone is wearing hard hats. We're feeling so proud to be part of the team that will create our miracle."

"Look, I gotta go," I said to Ron, "there's too much to do." I got up from my chair to leave.

"I'm staying, I've got groceries to buy," he said.

I hopped, skipped, and jumped to my car, with Ron watching me. I felt good driving back to work. Ron looked stronger and he said he had never felt better. I so much wanted him to get well and stay with us.

As for me, my mood changed from elation to terror every few minutes, it seemed. I loved making plans, but I was worried about paying for it all. Michael would dash over with swatches of fabric for the chairs, tables, and the rug. I always seemed to pick the most expensive ones.

One day I visited the architects' offices. Twelve chairs stood in a row. "Which one do you want? Make a choice."

I felt like Goldilocks. No, this chair is too small; no, this chair is too large. This chair is too hard, too soft, too high, too low. Ah, this feels just right.

"Diane," said Michael as he looked at me thoughtfully, "you've just chosen the most expensive chair, and you need 120 of them for the restaurant."

The budget kept climbing and I was climbing the walls. The first air-conditioning company, who had charged us $15,000, threatened to sue us for ripping out their work and replacing it with another system. Everybody wanted a deposit before the construction began. If I thought the air-conditioning bills were outrageous, they were nothing compared to the bill to get rid of the pillars.

The deadline for completion was February 18, 1994. That was the day the governor general of Canada was coming to cut the ribbon. If I'd had the ribbon in front of me now, I would have hanged myself with it.

The stars were selling well, but with the increase in the budget because of the cost of removing the pillars and the new air-conditioning unit, I was now short $600,000 to finish the project. I tried calling Ron for help, but there was no answer. The next day I went to meet him at the health food store, but he didn't show. I went to the pay phone and called him at home. This time his friend Don answered the phone.

"Diane, I'm sorry I didn't call you. Ron is in the hospital. They don't think he's going to make it."

"I can't believe this. He was looking great the other day. He said he'd never felt better in his life. How can this be?"

"He's at Wellesley Hospital. You can go and visit him there," Don said.

I hung up and cried. My best friend was dying in the hospital with cancer. I'd never felt so alone in all my life. Each day I sat at the edge of Ron's bed and told him, "Please hurry up and get better. I love you, I need you, and I want you to see this. Please, I can't do this without you."

"Yes, you can," he would say.

"I can't," I kept insisting. "Where will I ever get the money? I'm going to have a heart attack."

"No, you won't. Everything will be all right, I promise. Somebody will be there for you, you'll see." He held my hand.

"Ron, we started this dream together. You were always with me. It's hard, it's really hard. I'm afraid I'm going to fail."

"You won't fail," Ron said, as tears ran down my face.

Leaving the hospital each day I felt like a child about to lose a beloved parent. It was now time to grow up. I knew that Brent and Michael were doing a wonderful job, even though the fights between Michael and me over the budget increases were escalating.

"Oh my God! The taxes alone are crazy," I'd scream at him.

"Well that's not my fault! Go and yell at Brian Mulroney." Michael turned red as he stormed out of the room.

Benny assured me every day that the performers were not goofing off. Lesley was making sure everyone wore hard hats each time they went on the site.

Nearly every day I went to the hospital to see Ron. Each day he was failing, getting thinner and thinner.

One day, February 5, 1993, one year before the opening of our home, I felt awful. "I can't do this," I said to Terry, "I just can't go today. It hurts me to see him like this, I love him so very much."

"Don't go, Diane. Take a rest."

I tried to sit down at my desk, but I felt so guilty, I had to go. "Phil, I want you to drive me there, please."

"I don't want to go in, I don't want to see him like this. I want to remember him the way he was, always smiling and laughing at every crazy thing we did," Phil pleaded with me.

"No, I understand. Don't come in, just come with me."

We got in the car and drove to the hospital. When we arrived at the hospital, I took a deep breath before entering Ron's room. There he lay, quiet and still. Don, his friend, got up and said, "It's just a matter of time. Here, sit here and hold his hand and talk to him."

I sat down and said, "Ron, I love you. I love you a lot. The building is going to be great. We open this month next year. I want to present the Ron Secker Award in your honor to one of the players who with their sense of humor helped us all succeed. What do you think of that?" I paused. He was still breathing.

"I want you to present the award. They would love that. I love you, Ron."

He stopped breathing.

Quietness engulfed the room. It was as if the entire hospital, the machines and all the nurses and doctors had stopped. I felt as if the sun had gone inside me and filled me with love, a love for myself and others. I left the hospital and returned to where Phil was waiting for me. I didn't have to say a word. He knew. In silence, he drove me back to work.

The next morning was the first day of my life without Ron. I came to work and started to go through the faxes from Michael that had piled up the day before. Invoices, taxes, money, and more money. As I sat at my desk, I noticed an old birthday card that Ron had sent me.

My Darling Diane,

   You do give so much of your life to make so many people happy. You are loved and admired so very much. Everything will be all right.

Love, Ron

"Strange," I thought. "Where did this come from? How did it find its way to my desk? This was sent to me in September last year. What does this mean?"

I began to cry, but I felt strangely happy too. "Ron, you're still with me, I know you are. You couldn't miss the excitement of it all. Thank you for being here when I needed you." I returned to work, not feeling so alone, knowing that everything would be all right, that someone was watching out for me.

The phone rang. It was Ivan. "The trouble with you, Dupuy, is that you worry too much. I told you I was going to get the zoning approved. I told you the city wanted you to have a home. We had to make some minor technical adjustments, like it's to be called a performance workshop, an educational facility, but there's no need to panic or worry. Just get back to work and finish that building. I'm really looking forward to the opening ceremonies."

After talking to Ivan, another volunteer who takes his job with Famous People Players seriously, I realized that Ron was still with me.

12

"I Will Make You Cry"

Later that day, the mail arrived, delivered by Debbie Lim. As I shuffled through the pile of unpaid bills, I noticed a letter addressed to me. By the way the envelope was written, it appeared to be a person who was handicapped, or someone who had great difficulty writing. When I opened it, it read:

> Dear Mrs. Dupuy,
>
>   I've always wanted to meet you, ever since I first saw the Famous People Players perform at the John Bassett Theatre in Toronto. Your show has been on my mind for some time, and I'd very much like to visit you and meet you in person. I admire you and your work very much.
>
> Yours sincerely,
Sandy Mitchell

Within the next couple of weeks Sandy Mitchell came into my life. He was tall and balding, and he had the most delightful smile. He was full of a wonderful ray of light that came from within.

He was accompanied by Paul Sullivan. Both were wearing red sweatshirts bearing the name WindReach Farms. As they walked into my office, I noticed that Sandy's arm was limp, his hand was bent inward, his walk had a little hop, and when he spoke, he slurred his words. Sandy had cerebral palsy.

He smiled a lot as they asked me all kinds of questions. Why had I founded the Famous People Players? How difficult was it setting up a theater company? I kept telling him to read my book *Dare to Dream*. With my one deaf ear and his slurred speech, I had trouble understanding him. I was hoping that they would quickly get to the point and say what it was they were looking for. I gathered that Paul must have been the staff person who took care of him, so I directed my questions about Sandy to Paul, but Paul would always say, "Well Sandy, what do you think of that?"

Finally Sandy began to talk about himself. "I have a farm called WindReach, not far from Toronto. It's a farm for the disabled. I designed it myself. I have a hay wagon that can seat ten wheelchairs, so that everyone can enjoy farm life." As he spoke of his farm, he beamed with pride. The glow that came from Sandy brightened up our dark and gloomy rehearsal hall.

As I showed them around the space, I assumed that Sandy wanted the Famous People Players to give a benefit to help support his farm. I thought I'd break the ice and offer the services of our company.

"There you go, Dupuy, you can't raise any money for the Famous People Players, but you're going to help someone else raise money," a voice inside me warned.

"Sandy, Paul, perhaps you'd like to have the Famous People Players come and do a benefit for WindReach," I suggested.

They stopped in their tracks, laughed, and said, "Yes, maybe sometime. We'll see. We just want to know more about you."

Strange, I thought. Maybe they've been told we're box-office poison.

"Good luck with your dream. I know how hard it is to build something," Sandy said to me as he said good-bye.

As I watched them walk out the door, he turned and said the strangest thing. "You will be hearing from me. I promise I will make you cry, like you do when you're on stage." The door shut behind them.

"What did you make of that?" I said to Terry.

"I don't know, but what a nice man he was! His friend Paul was cute." We both giggled and went about our business.

Suddenly, we were interrupted by a surprise visit from Michael.

"Nothing can be done about the electrical system, the plumbing, the soil check, or the removal of the pillars, unless we receive a signed contract and a deposit of at least 20 per cent of the cost. There will also be a major delay on the construction because we have to get building permits. The final drawings have to be approved by the city planning department."

"The planning department! Not them again!" I groaned. Then I had an idea. "The Famous People Players are performing all summer in Quebec City. We'll be gone for two months. Perfect time for the construction to be happening."

"Well, brace yourself, it will be impossible."

A setback. I was still short $500,000 from realizing the dream.

I called my friend in Montreal, Joan Price Winser, who was once the Canadian consul-general in Los Angeles. We'd met her there in 1987 when the company gave a performance for songwriter and composer David Foster. At this gala event we'd also met comedian John Candy, who later donated money to us, and Bob Geldof, the rock star who'd raised millions for charity from the biggest benefit concert in the world, Live Aid. The gala was the first time that Joan had seen the Famous People Players perform and she was awestruck.

"If there is ever anything I can do for you, please don't hesitate to call," she had said.

Well, now I was calling, although she was no longer consul-general. I hoped she would remember me, and wouldn't mind my intrusion on her privacy. She was now living a quiet life with her husband in Montreal.

You can always recognize Joan's voice. It is a sultry, sexy voice, slightly hoarse from too much smoking. She often says, "I love to smoke. It's wonderful. I just love it. I can't think of my life without these wonderful cigarettes, taking a puff and inhaling."

I could hear smoke blowing into the phone. She sounded like Lauren Bacall. "Diane, it's wonderful to hear from you. Tell me, how are the Famous People Players?"

We talked for almost an hour, picking up where we'd left off back in 1987.

"I need a door-opener, Joan. You must know somebody who can give the Famous People Players some money. I was wondering about the Foundation. I submitted a proposal to them some time ago, on the original site. We have changed locations. The new place will be cheaper and perhaps they might reconsider." (Although I knew that if Michael came in with one more increase it wouldn't be cheaper.)

I left everything in Joan's hands. She still loved the Famous People Players. She promised she'd do everything she could to help me raise the additional $500,000.

"It's not a lot, Diane. We should be able to swing something."

I hung up, feeling a wonderful sense of hope.

"Well, what did she say?" I turned around to see Rossen standing beside me with her hand on her hip. "Well, what did she say? Did she remember us? Well, did she?"

"Rossen, how could she forget us?" I imitated her with my hand on my hip.

"Oh yeah? Now are you happy?"

"Yes, Rossen, I'm very happy."

"Wait till your mother and Terry hear about this. They'll be surprised," she said, her voice starting to sing.

"Debbie, let's go walk around and see what else we can sell to raise money. Maybe we can sell you." I laughed.

"Oh, you," she said, and put her arm around me.

Walking around the theater center, we kept looking for ideas. We had lots of windows in the restaurant area, and there were pillars down there too. We could sell these as Windows of Opportunity and Pillars of the Community for extra money to help pay for the construction cost.

"What about the floor?" Rossen suggested.

"No, it will be covered. Remember, Debbie, nobody's looking down." She sighed and nodded her head in agreement.

"Don't forget the seats in the theater," Mary reminded me. "You can sell those too," she said as she whisked by with Tina Turner's head in her arms.

There was no question about it. We had a lot of work ahead of us. Delaying construction until later in the summer made a lot of sense. This would give us more time to get our finances in order, apply for the building permits, and get a release on the government check. It would also give me time to approach different suppliers to donate products like the tablecloths and kitchen supplies, to keep the costs down.

Spring was here and the Famous People Players were booked for eight weeks of the summer in Quebec City at the Capitol Theatre in the old part of the town. Everyone was looking forward to a long-term run in one place, especially in a theater that had one of the best stages in Canada. Besides, we were all going to learn French and have a great time living in Quebec.

The new show would have some French numbers, and of course, a puppet of Quebec superstar Céline Dion. Her big hit in Quebec was "*Des mots qui sonnent,*" which translates into "Words that Ring." The lyrics of the song included lines about telephones ringing and the star being overbooked on TV and promotion shows.

While we were blocking the beginning of this number, Keith, Joanne, and Jeanine pretended to be Céline. Her puppet would take three people to bring it to life: Keith on the head and body, Jeanine on the arms of the puppet, and Joanne on the legs. Lisa and Lesley would be the telephone receivers. I started to direct them.

"We need microphones and cameras. They will have movable mouths and eyes. They will also be the back-up singers."

"Me, me, me, me," said Charleen, waving her arms in the air.

"Me too," said Michelle and Darlene.

"What are Ted and Gord going to be?" said Lesley.

"They'll be the gold records that float all around Céline as she sings."

"Okay, now when you hear the music, have Céline enter stage right, and strut across the stage to the center. Then the telephone people come on and hand her the phones to talk into. Sandra and Else, you pretend you're holding onto a long telephone cord and make it wave in the air."

"Sounds good," said Else.

Everyone loved the music and the fun of working on the Céline puppet. They pretended to move invisible objects in the air.

Another cute number we put together was called "Baby Jordy." A little five-year-old boy from France had recorded a hit song called *"Der der d'être bébé."* It's about a little child complaining that all his parents say is "Don't do this and don't do that." It was adorable with Lesley, Sandy, Else, and Michelle as baby ducks. Baby Jordy was going to be an ugly duckling and Darlene was going to be the baby bottle, while Jeanine would be Baby Jordy. The parents were two swans held by Ted and Gord.

Watching Mary and her creative team get to work on the creation of the best props ever was a delight from beginning to end.

Summer was almost here. In between the rehearsals for Quebec, we were able to sell a few windows and two pillars.

"It's too bad we have to get rid of the pillars upstairs," Charleen's mother said to me one afternoon, as we were loading up the props to go to Quebec.

"We could sell those too," Ted interjected. "Let's get people to give us money to take them down."

"Oh Ted, where would we put their plaque if there is no pillar?" asked Charleen.

"Don't laugh, Charleen. Ted has a great idea. We'll ask people to give us money to take away the pillars."

"Good idea," confirmed Michael.

"Good work," said Else.

"I'm sorry, Ted," said Charleen. "Now, Ted, you go get the money." Everyone applauded.

We were all very optimistic. A job for the summer would bring in a regular pay check and help carry the operating costs during the stressful times of creating our own theater center.

"When we come back from Quebec, will it all be finished?" asked Rossen.

"God, how I wish I could say yes, but no, it will just be beginning. You guys will only have a couple of weeks of rest, then it's off to the United States. When you come back, you'll see a big change. Not finished, but close to it."

The summer of 1993 in Quebec was the best summer I've had in years. Quebec is a beautiful city, with wonderful people. The food, the scenery, and the audiences were the best we have experienced anywhere. I know what touring Europe would be like by the way the Famous People Players were received in Quebec.

But the best thing that ever happened to me in Quebec wasn't receiving the rave reviews the company got, but the telephone call that came early one morning in my hotel room.

"Diane, it's Joanie Winser."

"You don't need to say who is calling," I said. "Your Lauren Bacall voice gives you away every time."

Joan puffed on her cigarette. "Look, darling, the Foundation wants you to know they hated the idea of that damn development property. They never liked the proposal, but they adore the concept of remaining right where you are. It is one hell of a smart idea, and I'm glad you did it. It will work. It's worth the investment. They are coming on board for $350,000. I know it's not much, but it is a start. Hello, hello? Diane, are you there?"

I couldn't speak. I was lying on the floor. I'd fallen off my bed when I heard the news.

"Diane, you sound out of breath."

"What can I say? I love you."

"Just do me a personal favor. Spend some time with your family. Take a rest and please don't worry. Everything is going to be all right. Also, the Foundation don't want anything to be named after them." She hung up.

"We've got the money," I ran down the hotel corridor from one room to another, banging on the doors, waking up the Famous People Players.

Gigglejuice was the first to open her door. She was wearing a purple nightie from Victoria's Secret. With one eye shut, she looked like Popeye in a nightie. "Well what do you say about that?" I imitated her voice.

She quickly responded, "Wait till Terry hears about this." Her voice grew louder with laughter as she was now wide awake.

Charleen came jogging down the hallway, rolling her sleeves up as if she was going to have a fight. "Well, what's the gossip?" she asked. When I told her she did her Zorro routine with me as if we had swords.

I immediately called Michael, and told him to get the ball rolling, we had the money.

It's funny how life takes these turns. You never know who you'll meet or what is around the corner. As I looked back on my journey down the yellow brick road, I could see even more clearly why everything hadn't gone right from the beginning. It was not the master plan.

The fall brought the autumn colors to Quebec and Ontario. The trees of red and gold, with their branches blowing in the wind, seemed to be singing Nat King Cole's hit, "Autumn Leaves." I must do this number in the show one day, I thought to myself as we drove back to Toronto.

As I watched the trees dance by, I realized more and more that my mind was not in control of me, I was in control of my mind. I will never again doubt my inner voice. Even when it comes up with a crazy idea or notion, I know it's right for me. All the answers are inside me. The power is in the moment, not yesterday, not tomorrow, but this moment, here and now. That's what those strong beautiful trees were saying to me.

How do you think we got this big, this strong? Live your life for the moment, that is where the power is. You will get to where you are going. There is no need to rush. Take it easy, and it will all come together.

It was true, a collection of little moments can create a big moment, just like a dripping faucet. One drop at a time is really nothing, but eventually it becomes a puddle. Keep thinking positive thoughts, one at a time, and you will eventually get rid of the negative thoughts. In the end, something big will grow from those thoughts.

I had so much to be thankful for. I had learnt so much on this journey. I felt inspired to ride my horse, Silver, and I could see Emerald City in the near distance.

As the company boarded the bus for another adventure across the American Midwest, I stayed at home to prepare for the construction workers who were starting Monday morning.

"We love you, Diane," said Rossen.

"Me too," said Lisa.

"Don't forget me and Sandy," said Lesley. "We love you too."

"And I love all of you. Ted and Gord, come here, and give me a good-bye hug."

"We're going to make you proud, scout's honor." They did their scout sign.

Phil Chart dashed over to say good-bye, after putting out his cigarette.

"It's great to be back on the road again. The adrenaline is pumping, man, and I'll give you a call once I clear the border."

"Who is going in the truck with you, now that Benny is staying to help me with the construction workers?"

"Greg. We're on our way."

Everyone was in a mad rush to get going. Phil would follow the bus in his Ryder truck.

Benny and I waved good-bye as we watched them head for the highway to Buffalo. Feeling alone, we climbed the staircase of our warehouse.

"Soon it won't be so rickety," Benny said.

"We have lots to do, Benny. We have to finish the opening plans. We have to learn how to cook if we are going to run a restaurant."

"And I'll make sure everyone wears a hard hat," he said, looking very determined.

The countdown had begun. Brent showed up before the cock crowed and the city had woken up. In less than four months we would have completed our dream, but a lot of work had to be done within these four months. The air conditioning, the electrical system, and the structural changes were the biggest and most time-consuming jobs of all. New windows would be needed for the prop shop. We had to make Anne McDougall proud. After all, they'd given us $75,000 for the Magic Room, and that came from a lot of hard work selling tickets to the Ottawa show.

The Magic Room is where Mary lives. I dropped in to see her. She was spray-painting and gluing props, turning pieces of foam into creatures that would make our performances come alive. Therese was trying to lift the octopus, which had been Joe Clark, up a ladder so she could hang it from the ceiling. The octopus with its eight tentacles took nine people to bring it to life on stage. Enrico put down his paintbrush to help her up the ladder.

"We need some more hands," he said.

Benny and Mary came to help.

Therese is petite, but tall in spirit. Her face is so beautifully shaped that we often tease her that being in props she must have designed her own face. Enrico, who comes from the Philippines, has a wonderful disposition. He's amazingly easy to get along with. When panic sets in, Enrico stays cool.

"We're getting new windows in here," I said.

"Are we also getting new prop tables with drawers?" Therese asked.

"I'm going to leave the prop shop to the three of you. You can supervise the construction workers in this area. Get the kind of prop tables you need."

"We need better ventilation for the dark room," said Mary. We walked into a small room that had no regular lighting. All that hung in this drab little room was a black light so Mary could see what type of fluorescent color she was painting. The room was fifteen by ten feet. It had paint cans everywhere and a huge spray compressor, which made a terrible noise.

"There's a window over here. I painted it black so I could have a dark room when I'm painting in black light. This is where we can put in a proper fan and ventilation system," she said.

"The lunchroom for the players will be great. John Candy gave us the money to do this and I want it to be perfect. We need cupboards, a fridge, a table, and chairs for the performers to sit on. Mary, that will be your project to supervise," I said.

"I know a nice carpenter who could do the job perfectly and who will work very cheaply. Else's dad is an electrician. We'll ask him to do the electrical work for the prop shop and lunchroom. That will save on the electrical bill for the architect," Mary said.

I faxed Michael and told him not to include the prop shop, lunchroom, and storage areas in his drawings and budget, because we were going to do that ourselves.

Each day on the construction site brought us new challenges to overcome. The deadline for the governor general's arrival was getting closer and closer. Michael and Brent both insisted they needed an extra three months to get things done.

"The ductwork for the air conditioning needs time and the weather is too cold to begin construction outside."

The weather was indeed cold. It was the coldest winter I could remember.

The major part of construction now shifted to the elevator for the disabled. Michael tried hard to figure out a solution to the installation.

"We got a steal on the elevator. The man who owns the company loves the Famous People Players and gave us the elevator for next to nothing. But now the bad news is the corridor. The wheelchair entrance will cost up to $100,000."

"More money?" I wailed.

"You have to make a decision if you expect to open February 18."

"What can I say? Do it. We have to go ahead, we cannot stop."

"Diane, we are at the mercy of the weather, it's too cold and the snow is coming down hard," said Brent one day.

I looked out the window and saw that the gently falling snowflakes had turned into a ferocious blizzard. The bad weather seemed to last for weeks. We were losing time. During this period, I felt like Dorothy asleep amongst the poppies. Time was passing, but everything had to wait.

By this time, Sandy Mitchell and I had become great friends. He'd visit me on the construction site and I'd visit him on his farm.

"One day, I'm going to make you cry," he would joke when I came to see him. "Cry for me, Diane."

"No, I won't." I ran ahead of him to the barn that housed goats, donkeys, lambs, deer, and pigs. Cold as it was outside, the barn was warm and inviting.

As we left the barn, Sandy pointed out, "Over there are my fruit trees. They are kept at a certain height, so people in wheelchairs can pick the fruit off them. In the summer, WindReach Farms is the most beautiful place to be on the face of the earth."

"It's funny," I thought, "when I first met Sandy, I had trouble understanding him. Now I know what he is going to say before he says it." There was no question about it, we were soulmates. We both had dreams. His was the farm and the people there, mine the home for the Famous People Players.

He walked me back to my car, which was covered in a foot of snow. We both started sweeping the snow off the window. I turned on the ignition to warm up the car for my drive back to the city.

"Sandy, I love WindReach, the countryside up here, even the snow. It's so peaceful. But at Famous People Players, this weather is going against us. I have to have that wheelchair entrance finished for the governor general's opening. My heart is in my throat. I even get nervous choosing textiles. All I see are sample swatches for the rugs and chairs. What happens if on the day we open nothing matches, everything is polka dots and stripes? I get scared that I might let everyone down. I don't want to fail."

"You won't fail," he said.

As I looked at him I found the determination to drive back to Toronto and take the bull by the horns. As I started to back out of the driveway, Sandy thumped at the window. I rolled it down and snowflakes blew in my face.

"I promised I would make you cry," he reminded me.

"I'll come see you next week. Pray for good weather," I said, leaving Sandy standing next to the dry patch where my car used to be, which was starting to get covered with snow.

No sooner had I got home than I entered into a new crisis. I have never seen Terry so angry. "You'll never believe in a million years what has happened."

"What's happened?" I said.

"Do you remember Geraldine?"

"Geraldine?"

"Geraldine, the blind girl that Tom and Kamile befriended last year."

"Of course," I said.

"You won't believe this. She went to the labor board and reported us for not giving her a full-time pay check for working with Famous People Players."

"You've got to be kidding!" I sank into my chair. "Wait a minute, I'm confused. I thought she was a volunteer."

"*You're* confused!" Terry said, waving Geraldine's file in the air.

"This doesn't make sense. She was a volunteer and this was a year ago. How can a volunteer claim she was a full-time employee?"

"That's what I said to Mr. Bully from the labor board."

"I'd love to know what brought this on. Why on earth would she want to do this to us after we were so good to her? And why is she coming forward a year later?"

"I'll tell you what brought it on," said Terry. "'Adrienne Clarkson Presents' aired last night and when she saw us on television I suppose she thought there was money to be had."

"What peeves me is that she's using her handicap to gain pity. It represents everything that I'm against."

"Diane, I'm not going to lose any sleep over this. I turned Mr. Bully over to Pat Anderson to deal with."

"Wait till Tom and Kamile hear about this!" I said. "They'll be really hurt."

"Worse, wait till our volunteers hear about this!" said Terry grimly. "Speaking of volunteers, Bruno is supposed to be in today to do the press kits."

That afternoon Bruno Calaminici came to report to work. After Terry and I explained what had happened, tears welled up in his eyes. "This is so distressing," he said. "It ruins things for the rest of us. If volunteers have to sign a contract before they come to a charitable organization to work, it will make them feel that the trust is broken before they start."

"I'm afraid that's what we're going to have to do from now on, Bruno. We'll have to get a release form signed by all volunteers that they are not expecting any remuneration."

"Whether they are volunteering their services or getting job training," Bruno added.

Bruno is one of the nicest people I know. Terry certainly couldn't have done without him, as he took his work at Famous People Players very seriously. He was always there when we needed him. We could count on him and he worked as hard as any full-time paid employee.

Other volunteers who have made a tremendous contribution to Famous People Players are Paula and Wally Neil. Whether it's loading a truck in forty-degrees-below-zero weather, or cleaning toilets, or taking out the garbage, or acting as ushers at our Toronto performances, they do it with pride. Paula has said on many occasions, "I get so much satisfaction from helping somebody else."

The phone rang. "It's Phil calling from the tour." Bruno pointed to the receiver for me to pick up.

"The shows are going great. We've had three standing ovations and they're going to have us back. But wait till I tell you what happened with Ted." He was laughing so hard he couldn't get the words out. "The bus was waiting for the light to change, when a car ran into the back of the bus. Everyone got off to take a look. Don't worry, it wasn't serious. Very minor.

"Lesley thought we should get a picture of this for the Famous People Players' album. So everyone starts rummaging through the luggage compartment looking for a camera. Most were out of film except for Charleen. She took the picture. Then we shut the luggage compartment and the bus started again. I was driving the truck and following them.

"It must have been twenty minutes before Else realized Ted wasn't on the bus. We thought we'd left him behind. So the bus pulled over. I pulled over too. I was worried that something was up. Greg and I got out of the truck and ran over to the bus.

"Else and Lesley told me they couldn't find Ted. Then we heard this thumping coming from underneath the bus. We opened the luggage compartment and there was Ted, sitting between the luggage and the barn door we use in the k.d. lang number. Can you believe it?"

We both laughed. "Gosh I miss you guys. I wish I was on tour. I miss the bus," I said.

"I miss Benny on tour," said Phil. "He usually gets me going when he puts his foot on the tailpipe of the exhaust of the bus and makes farting sounds. I'll never forget when his foot was there too long and the bus backfired. Benny was covered from head to toe in black soot."

"This is such a great break from the doom and gloom of fundraising," I said.

"How's the construction going?" said Phil.

"Well, the weather is slowing us down, but the inside work is going great."

"We'll be home in about three weeks."

I could hear the horn honking in the background for Phil. We quickly said our good-byes.

As I turned around I came face to face with Brent.

"We are taking the pillars down next week. We're ahead of schedule. The soil check was approved by the city and thanks to your friend Ivan, the permits have been approved. We thought we'd start this area now because it's too cold to work outside."

This was both good and bad news.

"Terry, we need more money! I don't dare ask Paul Newman. He's been so generous already. What if I write to Phil Collins? What do you think? Am I pushing it? I don't want to turn him off the company. Not everyone is a Newman in this business. Oh, hell, I'll write him anyway. Why not? He didn't come into our lives just to say, 'Hi, how are you? This place feels like home to me,' and then leave us in the lurch."

I sat down and wrote to Uncle Phil:

Dear Phil,

I hope I'm not pushing it or taking advantage of your good nature, but we've decided to build our home right where we are. I'm running into obstacles with the cold weather and I'm worried about completing the project for it to be ready in time for February 18. I'm going seriously over budget. I was wondering if I could ask you to underwrite the sound and lighting for the theater. I know it is a lot of money but if you could help us out we would all be sincerely grateful.

Enclosed is a budget and the type of equipment we need. I am not knowledgeable in this area. Any suggestions or recommendations are most welcome.

Thank you for your support,
Diane

I gave my letter a kiss before faxing it care of Annie.

"What would we do without fax machines?" Terry said.

I imagined it was in Annie's hands as we spoke.

Mary came in to the office. "Sandy Mitchell just called. He's coming with Paul Sullivan. He says he's got something very serious he has to tell you," she said. "You didn't make fun of him, did you?"

"Oh, Mary, stop it."

"I'm not kidding." Her eyes looked straight at me. "Jokes can get carried away. I bet you offended him," she said.

All night long I couldn't sleep. I knew Mary was right. Maybe Sandy was bringing Paul along to get up the courage to tell me that I'd hurt his feelings. Maybe he was mad at me because I told him to stop complaining and eat his wife's tuna casserole. Maybe, like a stupid ass, I'd forgotten to acknowledge his presence at a party when I was mingling with people. Oh damn, maybe that's what I did. I felt terrible. He probably thought I'd ignored him because he's handicapped. I tossed and turned in my bed.

"If you're going to jump around all night like a Mexican jumping bean, go sleep on the couch," Bernard complained. "I've got to get some sleep."

I took a blanket and pillow and headed down to the living room where I lay awake all night. The night has ways of playing tricks on your mind. I began to remember something that had happened when I was a little girl. A friend and I had been invited to spend the weekend with friends of my mother's. They were a childless couple, and the husband was handicapped. My girlfriend and I were both from broken homes and I think they felt sorry for us.

We had a great barbecue there and had lots of fun during the weekend. On the last evening we all sat around watching "Candid Camera," splitting our sides laughing. Then it was time to go to bed. The whole night long my girlfriend and I giggled. We told joke after joke, playing tricks on each other in our nighties. We jumped up and down on the beds, having the time of our lives. We took turns announcing, "You're on 'Candid Camera'!"

The next morning at breakfast, the couple seemed distant and quiet. Strange, we thought, we'd had such a good time the night before. The wife said good-bye and her husband drove us home, letting my girlfriend off first.

In the car alone, he turned to me and said, "You hurt me, Diane. I heard you last night in the bedroom laughing because I am crippled and have no legs. You and your girlfriend sat up all night long and made fun of me and my wife. I will never forgive you. After all we did for you, bringing you to our home."

I started to cry, "But we didn't. We were laughing and pretending to be on 'Candid Camera.'"

"Don't lie to me, Diane. I recognize that you have a vivid imagination. I will not be insulted. You are never welcome back in our house again."

He stopped the car and dropped me off at my house. I was devastated.

The sound of the snow hitting my windows told me that today I would cry, just as Sandy had said. I got dressed and left for work to face the music. Brent was there, feeling optimistic that the pillars would soon be removed and that would be one headache gone. Mary was making the lasagna, Benny was setting a nice table, and I waited for Sandy and Paul to arrive.

"Sandy and Paul are here," Terry said.

I got up nervously. I felt very anxious as I took them on a tour down the aluminum tunnel.

"Why are you so nice to me today?" said Sandy.

"Well, Sandy, I got to thinking that maybe I joke too much."

"You do," he agreed.

"Well, sometimes I forget people's feelings."

"That's true too."

"And maybe I haven't treated you with the greatest of respect and all."

"I agree with that," he said.

We sat down and I continued to talk.

"Before you start, I want to apologize if I've offended you. It was purely unintentional. I'm very sorry."

"I accept your apology, Diane. Now I promised to make you cry and I'm going to."

My eyes started to well up.

"I'm going to give you and the Famous People Players $100,000 to help pay for the elevator corridor."

I was stunned. Then put I my head on his lap and bawled like a baby. Still crying, I embraced him. I couldn't talk.

Mary came into the office, carrying the lasagna, with Benny behind her. "I knew it," she said. "She did something wrong. I've warned her. She's got to cool it."

Sandy looked up at her and said excitedly, "I made her cry, I made her cry. I gave the Famous People Players $100,000."

Mary almost dropped the lasagna. She put it on the table and went over and hugged him.

What a day, I thought, what a day. I was stunned. I didn't realize Sandy had any money. This came to me as a big surprise.

Watching Sandy and Paul walk toward their car in the snow, I remembered that show at the John Bassett Theatre, which was half-empty, and the lesson that we'd learned from Liberace. "You never know who's in the audience."

13

Countdown to Opening Night

The sun wasn't yet up and camera crews were preparing to film the pillars coming down. Brent had the construction workers lined up and ready to go for City-TV's "Breakfast Television" show. A zany host called Steve Anthony arrived to take his cue from an even zanier producer. Everyone was wearing a hard hat.

"We are going to wake up everyone in Toronto when these babies go," the producer told Brent, slapping the pillars with his hand. "We want it to look like our host is knocking them down."

Brent handed him the blowtorch and told him what to do.

"10, 9, 8, 7, 6, 5, 4 . . . stand by for live remote . . . 3, 2, 1 . . . action!"

"Good morning, Toronto! We're at the future home of the Famous People Players and you may not realize it, but it will be officially opened by the governor general of Canada on February 18. Now I'm going to bring down these big pillars you see here, to make way for the theater."

The cameras followed Steve around as he took down five pillars. Each pillar took twenty minutes to do. During the two-hour program, the feed went back and forth to the main studio, where the anchor was reading the morning news.

"Hope the building doesn't collapse," Steve said on the air to Brent.

"That would be one heck of a news story," Brent observed.

"I bring down the building and we all fall through the floor."

At this point everyone was laughing.

"Don't worry," Brent said. "Before you take the pillars down, you put in replacements. Structure beams." He pointed across the ceiling. "That's what's supporting the ceiling."

"Well, look at this room, it's huge," said the announcer when the pillars were gone.

I had to agree. Even though I'd lived and worked in this room for months, I couldn't believe it. Wait till Phil and the gang get back from tour, they're gonna die, I thought.

"That's a wrap. Good luck, Famous People Players. We at City-TV look forward to attending the opening."

The cameras shut down.

The snow had stopped falling, and Brent announced that they could now work outside. Hooray for us. Construction started on the wheelchair entrance.

It was all coming together. Then the phone rang. "It's Annie from England," Terry yelled from the office.

"Hello, Annie."

"Phil said yes. He's sending the check right away. But promise me you'll never tell anyone the amount. Phil wants to help you, but keep it quiet."

Annie was very excited. "I can't wait to see the place," she said. "Let me know how everything is working out."

Now that the pillars were gone, I could have done cartwheels throughout our big rehearsal hall. This is Phil's room, just like the restaurant is Paul Newman's, I thought. This will be the Phil Collins Performance Workshop. We'll name it in honor of Phil's wonderful visit, which gave us the inspiration and courage to look inside ourselves. Then I thought of Sandy Mitchell. I'd name the dining room WindReach in his honor.

Our home was starting to get a heart. The love of so many kind and generous people was becoming visible and taking shape around me. Greg's parents, Ed and June Kozak, paid for the elevator for the disabled. Close friends bought windows, pillars, and stars. And one of my most cherished friends left a very special mark on our theater. His name was Stephen Colhoun.

At that first meeting with Paul Newman in New York, I had asked Paul who had taken the wonderful photographs of him promoting his popcorn and spaghetti sauce. One of the best was of Paul sitting on a stool, holding up an umbrella, with popcorn raining down on him.

"That's one of my favorite photographers," Paul told me. "One of my closest friends, who lives just five minutes away from me."

I was touched when Paul later introduced me to Stephen. We met in a jazz bar in New York. Stephen, a tall, striking man in his late sixties, reminded me of some wild cowboy riding into the sunset. The moment we met, it was instant friendship. It was as if we were soulmates who'd lived another lifetime together, riding the prairies, robbing banks, and giving the money away to the poor. Our conversation seemed to pick up where we'd left off in another life.

Stephen and I laughed harder than I can ever remember laughing before, and shared a New York-style cheesecake with cherries all over it. He talked about the photographs he'd taken of some of the great stars of our century: Cary Grant, Jimmy Stewart, Marlon Brando. There were also many wonderful leading ladies, like my favorite, Audrey Hepburn. He was a master storyteller. His long arms moved as he described his first meeting with Paul Newman during the filming of *Exodus*.

"I'd love you to come to Canada to see the Famous People Players," I told him.

"Okay," he replied. "Let's go!"

So we took a flight to Toronto.

His wife, Mary, was just as interesting a character as he was. She'd been the flower-girl at Humphrey Bogart and Lauren Bacall's wedding. She accompanied the two of us as we hopped from one city to another, just like two cowboys following the Famous People Players on tour.

We spent a week in Albany, New York, with the company. Stephen took photographs of the players. I directed and Mary carried the tripod. We always seemed to be laughing.

"You're crazy, Dupuy," he'd say to me. "How does your husband put up with you?"

"How does Mary put up with you?" I shot back.

He blew smoke rings from his cigarette up in the air. Each one was bigger than the last. "Want to go to Africa?" he said. "We'll go on safari."

"Sure, when I'm not touring," I replied.

Stephen and Mary often came to visit us in Toronto. They took photograph after photograph and told wonderful stories. Stephen sat on my American board of directors and was always the center of attention.

"You know something, Dupuy?" he said. "I think you and I were at the O.K. Corral together." He took a sip of his martini, his favorite drink.

"If that's true," I said, "then I'm Wyatt Earp. And you, Doc Holliday (cough, cough), you smoke too much."

One afternoon when we were sitting in Toronto, he turned to Mary and said, "Let's go home, I don't feel so well."

A week later, he was diagnosed with cancer.

Instead of quitting smoking, he'd sit in his hospital bed in Connecticut, holding court, telling stories to the nurses as he sneaked a cigarette. Everyone loved the cowboy Stephen. Mary organized a dinner in his honor to be hosted by Jason and Lois Robards. I flew down as a guest of the Colhouns to spend what would be my last weekend, at least in this lifetime, with my wonderful friend and fellow traveler.

When I arrived, instead of seeing the strong athletic man who had been the best handball player at his club, I saw a thin, shriveled-up old man who had to be carried to the car to attend his awards dinner. Jason Robards, the host of the evening, said to me, "I love Stephen. I'm sorry I didn't know him longer."

Stephen died a few weeks later and the country's finest jazz musicians came to play at his funeral. It was a celebration of his life and the way he had touched all who knew him. Mary Colhoun took me aside and said, "Stephen would want you to have the original black-and-white photos that he took for the covers of *Look* and *Life* magazine for when you get your new home."

Brent constructed the bar that would be our tribute to Stephen. "I will call it Colhoun's Bar," I told Mary Colhoun, "because Stephen always liked his martinis straight up."

"If we don't have any more bad weather, I think we are going to make it," said Brent. "Each day is crucial. The painters start tomorrow and the rug is being put down next week. We are moving faster than humanly possible," he kept assuring me.

"There are so many last-minute things to do. Props have to be finished," said Mary.

"And invitations for the opening with the governor general have to go in the mail ASAP," said Terry.

"We need to order our china and silverware. We haven't done this yet. And you'd better hire a chef. I cannot build props and cook dinner for 150 people," said Mary.

"Who are we going to get to help us?" said Benny.

Here we are, opening a first-class restaurant and nobody knows how to cook, let alone serve, I thought. This was going to be like mounting a new production. Everyone had to be given a part and trained properly on serving and etiquette before we opened to the public. Famous People Players would have to take no work at all and concentrate on getting ready for the opening of the theater center. We must create a meal as good as our performances for the governor general.

"CNN called from New York. They're covering the event!" screamed Terry.

"The *New York Times* and Associated Press reporters are coming too. We'd better deal with this cooking issue. We do not want anyone saying that the food is lousy. Newman would kill me," I said.

Ronnie Brown, a staff performer, recommended that I call one of the best restaurants in Toronto, Alice Fazooli's. He once worked there and knew the owners. One of the owners, Rick Montgomery, came to our rescue with his number-one chef. The two of them advised the architects on kitchen design and sat with me to plan easy and efficient menus that even I could do.

Rick, one of three partners of many great restaurants, is an easy-going guy with a delightful sense of humor. He's one of the people who brought the game Trivial Pursuit to the world, Terry told me.

"Rick, there should be something on Famous People Players in that game."

"You're right, Diane, but we don't have anything to do with it anymore. We're in the food business now."

They walked around the construction site where our restaurant would soon stand.

"I think what you should do," said Rick's chef, "is get in touch with Humber College. They run a culinary school here in Toronto. They have some wonderful students who I'm sure would jump at the chance to get involved with Famous People Players."

Rick took this idea even further. "Then once they've been through the program here at Famous People Players with your performers, we would be willing to give them a job at one of our restaurants." He also gave us a generous check from Alice Fazooli's restaurant.

I was so excited by their idea that I immediately acted on their suggestions. I sent a fax off to Humber College to see if the instructors could help us out with training. I also suggested that the Famous People Players could be part of a cooperative credit course for their students.

Within forty-eight hours I had a great response and the Humber College people were on our doorstep. Looking around at the half-finished kitchen, John Savard, the instructor from Humber, made some helpful suggestions about how to improve on the design.

"What kind of things do you want to cook?" he said to me.

"Things that are easy, like lasagna, beef stroganoff, prime rib, chicken *cordon bleu*. Anything that can be cooked in the oven. No deep frying. We'll be using Newman's Own Products, such as his salad dressing for our house salad, spaghetti sauce for the lasagna, and popcorn for the children. However, we are open to suggestions."

"You'll need to get two people to train the players on proper etiquette, like how to set a table, and serve food. Then you'll need someone who knows how to order food, a purchasing agent. Proper equipment has to be ordered for the kitchen—a microwave, conventional oven, pots, pans, utensils, meat slicer, food processor, and the right ovens. Also, you'll need someone in charge of the bar. There's the uniforms, tablecloths, napkins, and all the bar equipment—glasses, shakers, bar trays, ice-makers, glass-washer, a fridge for the bar, ice-scoops, condiments, and, of course, the booze. Most important of all, you need a chef."

I was speechless. I hadn't realized that what I'd planned was going to be so complicated.

"I want everyone to volunteer their services. I want the parents to be the bartenders."

"Diane, we will give you our students for six months full-time to get you up and running, but training the performers should have started a year ago. There's so much to learn. I don't think the same people can perform and serve in the dining room. You don't want kitchen workers to be sweaty. You'll need new people to join the Famous People Players."

It was time to open the company to new people to learn and be part of the magic. Immediately Terry pulled a file of letters from people who had written us to ask about letting their children join the Famous People Players. We lined up appointments with Mary, who always did the interviewing.

"I do the interviewing," she said to the first candidate, a young Asian girl called Ginny Young, "because everyone who joins the company works first in the prop shop. They learn all about the props and how to take care of them, and then Debbie Lim will teach you how to run errands all over Toronto. It's a lot of hard work before you can become a performer."

Ginny kept her head down. "I want to join," she said, "I want to train."

"First, you'll have to learn to look me straight in the eye, and sit straight. Don't slouch in the chair."

Ginny straightened up a little and looked at Mary out of the corner of her eye.

"You're accepted," Mary said. "You start Monday morning, nine a.m."

Ginny smiled with relief.

Next came a young man by the name of Josh Balanaser. He practically knocked us over with his enthusiasm.

"I love the Famous People Players. I saw your show at the Canadian National Exhibition last year, and I said to my mom, 'I can do that, I want to do that.'" Mary was struggling to get a word in edgewise. "I like you, I want to be in the company," he kept saying.

"Well, in order to be in the company you have to work for me in the prop shop, be on time, learn to listen, and not do so much talking."

"Okay, I'll do that. I want to do that."

"Okay, Josh, you start Monday morning."

The last candidate we accepted was a girl by the name of Cynthia Smith. She sat there quietly with her mother.

"There's nothing wrong with Cynthia except that she's a little slow. Other than that, she is fine, not like the others you have in this company," said Cynthia's mother.

"Don't underestimate the others," my mother told her fiercely. "You'd be surprised. Reading and writing doesn't make anyone any better. It's learning to work as a team that's important. Having a superiority complex is a bigger handicap than anything else."

"You tell 'em, Mary," I thought.

The mother shrank a bit and let her daughter talk to Mary.

"I can do all this," she said. "Can't I, Mother?"

"Cynthia, in Famous People Players we don't get our parents to answer questions for us. You are applying for this job, not your mother."

"Oh, I see," she said. "I'm sorry."

"That's okay, we all do this in the beginning. If you start in the Famous People Players, you will work for me in the prop department first, then if you do well there, you'll work with Diane in the rehearsal hall and learn to become a performer in the company."

"I'd love that," she said. "I'll try."

"Good, you start Monday morning at nine. Don't be late."

"I won't."

As all three candidates left, Terry, Mary, and I looked at each other.

"There's going to be a lot of work with all of them," I said. "I think Cynthia's mother needs to learn a lot about us. I just hope Cynthia can take all the discipline that goes with being in the company."

Sometimes parents don't want to accept the fact that they have a child who is handicapped. They make up one excuse after another as to why their children can't do certain things.

Monday morning arrived, and Josh was on our doorstep at seven, wildly excited about his first day in the Famous People Players.

Cynthia's mother drove her to work.

"Mrs. Smith," I said as I went over to her car, "in Famous People Players, it's important that everyone get themselves to work on their own. We are trying to teach them independence. I know you work at the other end of town and you've gone out of your way to bring Cynthia here."

"I wanted to make sure she wasn't late," she explained.

"Don't worry about her being late. It's all part of the learning experience. The players have to do things like make their own lunches, because when they go out on tour they don't have their parents, they're on their own and we want them to be very prepared to handle things on their own."

She thanked me and drove off.

"Don't worry," a voice came from behind me. I turned around and saw Benny. "I'll help her, I promise." We walked up the stairs. It was now nine o'clock and Ginny had not yet arrived.

❄

The deadline was getting closer and closer. Terry was putting the invitations in the mail. Mary, Therese, and Enrico were still designing the Magic Room.

When the performers arrived home from tour, there was no time to unpack. They were whipped off the bus and into the John Candy lunchroom to start training with a young student from Humber, Jason Morgan. Jason was only twenty-one but he had all the aplomb of the top maître d' at the Plaza in New York. However, before he could start training them, the players had to look at the changes to the building.

"Look at the rehearsal hall," screamed Lesley.

Everyone ran in.

"Oh my God," Charleen gasped.

"I don't believe it," said Phil.

"Diane, what happened?" Michelle's eyes were huge.

"The pillars are gone," said Gord to Ted.

"Yeah, I took them down with one karate chop," said Benny.

"You can hear an echo," said Greg, and he started to yodel.

"Come on, guys, we need to rehearse serving," Jason said.

They trooped back to the lunchroom, where Jason had laid out my dinner plates, stemware, and cutlery from home.

The next Humber student to arrive was a slim black woman about twenty-nine years old, by the name of Carol Clarke. She would be our purchasing agent. "We're ordering all the equipment this afternoon for the restaurant," she told me.

Brent was running around like a madman with someone who was supposed to install the fire alarm. "Get Ivan on the phone, quick! We need the building inspector to approve the accessibility before we can get the occupancy permit."

"Out of the way," the painter said. "I'm coming through. Don't walk on my tiles. This area is out of bounds. You have to go around." This meant we had to use the side door and run around the front of the building, which was two blocks long.

Losing rehearsal time to get ourselves ready was a tough decision, but there was no time to worry about what to do.

"The ceiling can be painted black, which will save money, but if you really want something absolutely stunning, you could install a fiber-optic ceiling," said Michael.

"What the hell is a fiber-optic ceiling?" I asked, as I rushed into the rehearsal hall.

"It's a surface covered with tiny lights that change colors, almost like a wave effect," he replied, moving his hand up and down to show me. "The colors go from blue to yellow to pink to red. Go see the lobby of the SkyDome Hotel. They have one there."

"How much is this going to cost me?" I glared at him.

"I think I can get it for a good deal."

"What do you consider a good deal, Michael?"

"Oh, about $25,000."

"$25,000! Just for light that changes color!"

"Look, Diane, it's up to you. You decide. I'm just telling you the price. Keep the ceiling black and save money, if you prefer."

"Money. I wish everything didn't cost so much money. Now you've got me looking at the ceiling and feeling that it will look awful if it's just painted black."

"It won't look awful. It's just that if you really want something stunning, then fiber-optic is the way to go."

"I'll think about it. When do I have to let you know?"

"If you want it installed in time for the opening, then I'll have to know by the end of December. It'll have to be designed and built to order."

"Diane!" A big yell came from the rehearsal hall. It was Ginny. She and Else ran up to me.

"Ginny was short-changed at the greasy spoon up the street," Else said. "She gave the man $10 for a cup of coffee and all she got back was $2. See?" Else took Ginny's hand and showed me the money in it.

"I didn't know," Ginny said sheepishly.

"Else, Ginny, everyone! Get over here, right away! I want to have a meeting with all of you! Come into the rehearsal hall! Now!" I hollered.

Everyone gathered around me quickly.

"I've told you once. I've told you twice. I've told you a hundred times: Stay away from the greasy spoon up the street! Ginny just got short-changed there. This isn't the first time it's happened and it won't be the last. I'm sick and tired of having to drop whatever I'm doing to go up there to fight for your money back. Now, Ginny, you're new here, I know. But yesterday I heard Joanne telling you not to go there for lunch."

"I didn't go for lunch. I went for coffee. That's all."

"Don't go there at all. For anything. Ever."

"What about my money? Now I've got no money for the subway. How am I going to get home tonight?"

"You have $2 in your hand right now. That's enough to get you home. I am not going to go to the greasy spoon and get in another big fight with the owner. I have had it with him. I don't want it to happen again. It's time you learned to handle your money better. I want you to sit down with Joanne right now. She will teach you how to count your money."

"I can't count very well."

"Well, my girl, you're about to learn. After all, you can't go through life hoping that everyone will give you the right change."

"I'll teach her," offered Darlene.

"Me too!" said Else.

"What about me, Diane?" asked Ted. "Can I help too?"

"Everyone can take an hour off rehearsal and Joanne will lead the class. Everyone can help. But remember, nobody from the Famous People Players is to go to the greasy spoon again. Not under any circumstances. Understand?" I wagged my finger at them.

"But I want my money." Ginny started to cry.

"How old are you, Ginny?" I asked.

"I'm twenty-six," she whispered.

"Stop looking at the floor. My face isn't down there. It's up here." I put my hand under her chin and got her to look up at me. "Twenty-six years old and you're crying about your stupid money. Go fight your own battle with the owner if you want it back. You're an adult. Go and do it."

"I don't want to," she said a little more loudly.

"I want you to. Why should I have to go? It's not my money. I didn't go to the greasy spoon. I wasn't the one who didn't count my change. No, Ginny, you have to go and fight your own battle."

"But I'm scared," she whined.

"Scared of what? He isn't going to hurt you. You just tell him that if he doesn't give you your money back, you'll call the police."

Ginny stared at me intently. She seemed to be thinking hard.

"Okay, I'll go," she said finally.

"I'll go with her," said Benny.

"Me too," said Ted.

"Okay, all of you go and let me know what happens. But I want you to understand one thing: The owner of the greasy spoon has done this before and he will do it again. Don't give him your business. If you insist on going there, be prepared to suffer the consequences."

"What does 'suffer the consequences' mean?" asked Darlene.

"It means that something will happen that you won't like. Now all of you go with Joanne and learn about money. And next time, think before you give it to someone. Okay?"

"Okay!" they chorused.

"Ten four!" said Gord as they headed back to the lunchroom with Joanne.

When I turned around to finish my conversation with Michael, he had disappeared.

The SkyDome Hotel, I thought. What the hell. It won't hurt just to take a look.

As I ran back to the office, Lesley called out to me, "Your shoelaces are untied! You'll fall!"

I stooped down to tie my laces when I reached Terry's desk, half out of breath from running. "We need an escalator in this place, it's so big," I panted. "Now get your bag, we're going to the SkyDome Hotel."

"Why are we going there?" Terry said, looking up from her computer.

"I'll tell you in the car. Turn off your computer and meet me in the parking lot."

As we drove there, I told her what Michael had said. "When we get into the lobby, just look up."

The doorman must have wondered about us as we came through the revolving door with our heads back and our faces aimed at the ceiling.

"Look at it!" I whispered in awe to Terry. "Isn't it beautiful? And it belongs at the Famous People Players theater, not here. I wonder if they'd give it to us. It's perfect."

Terry started to chuckle. "They are not going to give you their ceiling." She grabbed my arm and tugged me away from the lobby.

"We've got to raise the money. I want that ceiling."

"You've hit everyone up for money. There isn't any left, and we're way over budget. As for the bills in the drawer, I can't shut it anymore."

As we drove away I turned to her and said rudely, "Well, start another drawer. I'm going to get that ceiling if it kills me."

As soon as we were back on the construction site, the saga of Ginny and her money continued.

"Diane, the owner of the greasy spoon won't give her her money back," Ted and Benny told me. "He told us to call the police."

"Tell Diane what you said, Ginny," said Benny.

"I told him that I'll never come to his restaurant again."

"Me too," added Benny.

"And I told him that no one from the Famous People Players will ever come back. No french fries or hamburgers for us. I told him he'll lose a lot of business."

"Good for you, Ginny. I'm proud of you for standing up to him."

"Look," she said, "if I buy a cup of coffee, Joanne says that I should only give the cashier a loonie and not a bill until I learn my money better."

I took her hand. "Ginny, you hold your hand out longer, look them in the eye, and pretend you are waiting for more change. When you're not sure, fake it."

"Okay, I'll fake it."

"Ginny." I put my arms around her. "One day there will be no Famous People Players around to help you and you'll be on your own. That's why it's so important for you to learn right now how to take care of yourself."

"I love you, Diane Dupuy," said Ginny. She gave me a big squeeze.

"I love you too. Now get back to work and learn your parts in the show."

"Ten four!" she said, mimicking Gord with a high five as they all left the office.

I turned back to my messy desk. There were papers everywhere, mostly invoices, dozens of them strewn over the top. I grabbed them, bundled them up, and stuffed them in another drawer. "I've got to have that ceiling," I muttered. "I just have to figure out how."

Catherine McCartney, a dear friend of mine for the past twenty years, is considered the best Canadian agent and manager in the business. She represents Canadian actors like Al Waxman and used to represent the late John Candy. Catherine, I thought, she'll know someone who would like to give us twenty-five grand for a fiber-optic ceiling. I picked up the phone and dialed.

"*McCartney Enterprises. Please leave a message after the tone.*"

Damn. I slammed down the phone without leaving a message. I thought some more. Uncle Phil. I'll fax him and see if he can introduce me to Michael Cohl.

Michael Cohl was just getting ready to produce the Rolling Stones tour and he seemed the perfect candidate for the ceiling. His company, CPI Entertainment, was responsible for bringing stars like Phil Collins, Elton John, and Rod Stewart to perform at the SkyDome.

I faxed England and got an immediate response. Phil wrote to Michael Cohl and faxed me a copy of his wonderful letter.

Annie added a note: "Can't wait to see you at the opening. Good luck."

I faxed Phil's letter to Catherine. On the cover sheet I wrote, "You are IMPOSSIBLE to get hold of, wheeling and dealing with all those stars. Please wheel and deal for me. Follow up the attached letter from Phil Collins. You know all those great people at CPI. HELP! Love, Dora."

Christmas was another delay. "Holidays, we can't take holidays!" I cried to Brent. "Each day is precious."

"Diane, the men need to be with their families. I'm going to tell you right now, we are not going to be finished on time. It's impossible."

We sat down to assess the situation.

"Okay, let's look first at the air conditioning," said Brent.

"We can do that later, it's winter, we won't be using it," I said, "but Brent, everything else must be finished and on time."

Christmas came and went. Every day Benny carefully watched all the construction workers to make sure they didn't goof off. But he needn't have worried about them.

"Diane, they're Italian, like my dad," Benny told me. "They work hard till they sweat."

Benny helped lay the plywood on the stage, which would eventually be covered with a special flooring.

"Benny, I need you to deliver this parcel for me," Terry said.

"I can't, I'm helping Brent to take out the garbage and put it outside in the bin. There's lots of garbage from all the men's work. The rug comes tomorrow and I have to be here. I'm busy, you'll have to find somebody else."

"I need someone to deliver this parcel," Terry said desperately, as she ran from one person to another. The performers were strutting around with trays and glasses. *Crash!*

"Oh, God, my glasses," I moaned.

Throughout the day I heard bangs, crashes, and swear words from everyone. I lost my entire set of dinnerware. We had to eat off paper plates at home.

"Don't touch the wall," the painter said, as everyone had an impromptu class in fingerpainting.

"We can't read your sign," said Else.

"And Debbie Lim can't see so she has to touch the walls to find her way, so there," said Rossen.

"The new people, get the new people, they're moving too slow," yelled Benny to Else who was across the room finishing rehearsal.

"I'm trying," she said.

"Come on, Cynthia, hurry up. Put your prop away. We have to practice serving tables with Jason."

"Stop telling me what to do," Cynthia snapped.

"I'm only trying to help you."

"I don't need any help."

"We all need help," Else said, almost in tears.

"I'm tired of all the rehearsals. They're so long and I don't like staying late and rehearsing" Cynthia huffed as she stalked away.

"Cynthia, stop," I called out. "Wait just one moment before you walk away from Else. I want you to sit down and listen to what I have to say."

"I will not." She stamped her foot and stormed out of the building.

"I'll go after her," said Else.

"That's very nice of you, but let her go home and cool down. We'll talk to her tomorrow."

"Josh and Ginny are okay, Diane. I'm helping them, but Ginny is always late for work, and Josh is always banging into everyone. Last night on the way home, the doors of the subway opened and he pushed everyone aside when he went through the doors. I'm trying to train him to wait till everyone gets off the subway. It will take time, Diane," Else said with a sigh.

The order went in for the dinnerware. It was to be bone china, with a design of a top hat and cane, made specially for us in England.

Finally all the kitchen equipment arrived. John Savard came along with our new chef, a twenty-three-year-old student with a huge smile. D'Arcy Moffat was to become a very important person in the realization of our dream.

"Mr. Newman is a friend. I cannot let him down. The food must be perfect," I told D'Arcy.

"No problem." It was one of D'Arcy's favorite phrases.

"Guess what? D'Arcy smokes like a fiend," said Phil delightedly. "Now I'm not alone. Welcome aboard, D'Arcy."

The two shook hands.

"Oh God, not another smoker. Why is it that I always attract smokers?"

Cynthia rang the next morning. "I quit. I don't want to come back," she said on the phone.

"Cynthia, you are a lovely lady with very special qualities. You are polite to people, you conduct yourself with confidence. It was for these reasons we chose you to join the Famous People Players. You have not only let yourself down but the team you work with."

"My mother doesn't like you and the Famous People Players. You make us work too hard, and the rehearsals are too long."

"Did you tell your mother that the reason for the long rehearsals was because you were new and everyone has to work with you to make sure you understand what you are doing in the show? I know it's hard to face your responsibilities, but we all have to do it. People respect someone who can sit down and talk calmly, maturely, and professionally about job stress or the difficulty of working with co-workers. Three times a week we have our meetings and everyone is asked if there's a problem. Last week you said, 'No, I'm very happy here and very excited about the restaurant.' You told me when you were at your locker getting ready to put your uniform on, 'I can't wait till my mother sees me in this.' We didn't quit on you when you didn't show up for your parts on stage or when you came out backward or when you fumbled and dropped the props on stage. We didn't call your mother when you did things wrong. You are twenty-one years old and we dealt directly with you and treated you like an adult. Don't let yourself down, Cynthia. Come in and discuss the problems you're having. It's nothing to be ashamed of. We're here to help. Let's work together."

"I'm not coming in. I don't like you or the Famous People Players. I'm not like them. God, they're so stupid, always forgetting their parts in the show. My mother says I don't have a handicap." She hung up.

The trouble with this world is that nobody ever thinks they have a handicap, when in fact we all have handicaps to overcome. As for Cynthia, her handicap was believing she was perfect. What a waste of human potential.

The phone rang again. "It's Josh's mother," said Terry. "Last night Josh walked home in below-zero weather. He wasn't wearing his cap and he got frostbitten on his ears. He won't be in for a few days. He's going to the doctor."

"This is going to slow down his training" I was almost ready to throw in the towel when the phone rang. It was Catherine McCartney.

"You've got it!" she said excitedly. "Michael Cohl will cough up the money for your ceiling! He's getting ready to launch the Rolling Stones worldwide and because of his relationship with Phil Collins, whom he admires tremendously, he'll give you the money. The plaque is to read: "The Entertainment Centre, paid for by CPI Entertainment." After the opening, he wants to come down with his children and see the place. His company is interested in having after-hours parties at the dinner theater for rock stars when they come to perform at the SkyDome. So be happy, Dora Doom! You ought to be Dora Delight after this news!" She hung up.

I quickly called Annie in England to tell her the good news. "Tell that boss of yours that when he dies, he is going straight to heaven. We love him dearly."

Annie laughed and said, "Give our love to the group. I can't wait to come to Toronto to see you all."

As soon as I had finished talking to her, I called the architect's firm and asked for Michael. "The ceiling! We've got the money for the ceiling! I want it for the opening."

"Diane, this is the middle of January. The opening is in three weeks. I told you to let me know in December."

"I've got to have that ceiling!" I started to cry on the phone. "The donor wants it for the opening. If I don't get it, I'll lose the donation. Do anything you can to get it for me."

Terry looked at me with what Jeanine calls her Betty Boop eyes. "You're not going to lose the donation, you know." She laughed.

"I know. I just had to do something to get them working on it really fast."

But the place was taking shape. For one thing, the aluminum tunnel was no longer aluminum.

"Solid as a rock," said Michael cheerfully. "It looks great. Don't you love it?"

I didn't recognize it was the same tunnel. It didn't even look like a tunnel anymore, it looked like a gorgeous entrance to the theater. The rug was laid in the theater and it woke up the barren room. Phil hung the newly made black velvet drapes and the sound system was installed.

"The windows! Look at the new windows in the prop room!" Mary exclaimed.

We all stopped working for a moment. With our arms around each other we gazed out of the huge picture windows.

"Anne McDougall would be so proud," I said.

The press was arriving for interviews and everybody was excited.

"Paul Newman can't come, as he is making a new movie called *Nobody's Fool*, but he's sending the vice-president of Newman's Own, Ursula Hotchner. Phil is sending Annie, since he will be on tour. John Candy is sending Catherine McCartney," said a frazzled Terry. She had one pencil behind each ear and one holding her hair together.

"They're here in spirit, all of them," I said.

"Mary Colhoun is coming from Connecticut. She wants to hang Stephen's pictures on the wall herself."

The countdown was at ten days and those days were going fast.

"Oh, for God's sake, we've run out of photocopy paper. Somebody has to pick up the picture frames for Ron Secker's Memory Lane, and they have to be fast," said Terry frantically.

"I'll go," said Debbie Lim.

"There is too much for you to carry, you'll need to be driven. Phil will take you," Terry said as she ran to get the car keys.

"I can't go, I'm working the sound. It's got to be right. After all, this is called the Phil Collins Workshop."

People ran up and down the stairs, up again, down again, around the building, on top of the building, behind the building. We were like chickens with our heads cut off.

"The lights, we have to turn the lights on."

"They're installed. And the wheelchair entrance is finished," yelled Brent.

"Move!"

"Hurry up!"

"Let's go!"

"The bathroom, I have to go to the bathroom."

"No time."

Carol handed me a bill for the kitchen equipment. I put it in my desk drawer. D'Arcy handed me a bill for the food. I shoved it in the drawer. Terry gave me the mail, which was full of unpaid bills. Into the drawer they went. Mary gave me the bill for windows. Into the drawer. Eventually the drawer wouldn't close.

"Josh and Ginny are ready to perform," said Jeanine, sounding exhausted. "Ginny will be bringing your stool on and off stage in the dark and Josh will do the baby duck in the "Baby Jordy" number. It took us a month to train them to do it. I just hope they don't forget. And Else has come a long way, she helped them a lot in the wings."

Finally it was just two days before the opening.

"Diane, it's Ursula Hotchner. I'm in Toronto early. I have something for you from Paul, where can we meet?"

"I'm picking up Mary Colhoun tonight, so we'll both meet you at your hotel for lunch tomorrow."

"Perfect," she said.

That night I met Mary Colhoun at the airport.

"Mary."

"Diane."

We embraced, not letting go of each other.

"Mary, we're running out of time."

"Well, put me to work."

Mary and I worked until one o'clock in the morning, hanging Stephen's pictures all around the bar, while two volunteers and friends of Ron Secker's hung the photos of the Famous People Players for his Memory Lane. There was no time to say "How are you doing?" "How's your health?" "How are you managing?" to anybody. We just worked and spoke only in shorthand.

The next day we tore off like Newman on a race track to meet Ursula, a young Swedish woman who was married to the writer A. E. Hotchner, Paul Newman's best friend.

"Paul wanted to be here, but he is making a movie and thank God for that, because that means he's making money. He wanted me to give you this. He thought you could use it."

She handed me an envelope. When I opened it I was flabbergasted. A check for U.S. $30,000 was inside.

"Paul appreciates the hard work you must be doing on the construction. He built Camp Hole in the Wall for children with cancer. He knows all about construction overruns."

"God bless him, God bless him," I kept saying over and over. After all he had given to Famous People Players this was totally unexpected.

"I'm dying to see the place," she said.

"Oh my God, I have to go, we aren't ready yet."

Mary set a land-speed record getting me back to work. She had once been a pilot for Richard Nixon, and I think she had forgotten that she was driving a car, not a plane.

When we arrived we couldn't get any attention from anyone. The place was crawling with Royal Canadian Mounted Police officers doing security checks for the governor general. Phil was working on the sound. Enrico was finishing the paint job on the new prop tables and Mary was spray-painting in her newly ventilated spray booth. Terry was like a mad dog at her computer. Brent was up on a ladder yelling at Terry to get Ivan on the phone. "We need the building inspector

back here to approve the elevator so we can get our liquor license."
The electrician was running around with extra cables. D'Arcy and his
staff were preparing for the luncheon with the governor general, and
all the performers were in the restaurant with Jason practicing serving the guests.

The fiber-optic ceiling was being installed. "I'm working all night,"
the man at the top of the twenty-foot ladder told me. "The ceiling
will look beautiful. To tell you the truth," he winked, "it's much nicer
than the one in the SkyDome Hotel."

Suddenly, I decided to take a breather. Mary Colhoun and Terry
joined me at Colhoun's Bar for the first drink. It was then that I realized what had happened. I looked up and saw Emerald City—
Newman's Own Kitchen with its black awning hanging over the
entrance, the Art Deco ambience of the WindReach Room, the silver blinds, the black and gray tables and chairs, and the lights hanging over each table. The rug had the blueness of Paul Newman's eyes
and Stephen's photographs gave the room its finishing touch. The
light box that lit up our logo, the top hat and cane, stood in the center of the room. The entrance doors were decorated with Liberace's
name, piano, and candelabra. I slowly got to my feet. Choked up, I
turned to Mary and Terry.

"We did it. We actually did it. We made a dream come true. I can't
believe it, we made a dream come true."

Then I saw a sight that I will never forget as long as I live. Else,
the girl who shook so much when she first joined the company she
couldn't even hold a prop in her hands, who on her first tour with the
company couldn't even unlock the door to her hotel room with her
key, was practicing carrying a tray piled with champagne glasses. She
was walking back and forth with her head held high, and she wasn't
shaking at all.

"Very good, now smile," Jason instructed her.

Ted and Gord were following her, proud as peacocks.

"Diane," Brent said, interrupting my thoughts, "I need to know
where you put all of the unpaid bills."

"Not now, Brent. Can't you see a dream, a wonderful dream, has been realized?"

I looked around. Terry was crying. I was so elated, I swear I was flying. I opened the door to the stairway to the stars and saw a plaque that said "All of us are in the gutter, but some of us are looking at the stars."

I walked up the stairway where Mary, Therese, and Enrico had just finished putting the last stars up. Names that probably don't mean anything to anyone else meant a lot to me. Pat Anderson, Judi Schwartz, Gord Swayze, Catherine McCartney, the Kozaks, Debbie Rossen, Iris Billinger, the Lim family, Barb Tuckwell, the Brown family, and so many others.

We were still missing a patron to name the Stairway to the Stars after.

"I don't care how desperate I am for money," I said to Terry, "it has to be someone very special—as special as the people who gave these stars, the real stars."

At the top of the staircase was Memory Lane, the memorial to Ron Secker. There was a picture of Liberace and Tony Orlando, and one with Paul Newman and Joanne Woodward backstage with the Famous People Players. There was Lorne Greene, my first chairman of fundraising back in 1977. I smiled. Reviews after reviews.

I walked down the lane, surrounded by memories and pictures. Lights shone down on the pictures, and twinkling lights outlined the arches in the lane. Then the end of the tunnel appeared before me. The Phil Collins Performance Workshop.

Phil Chart was dancing to his sound system. The seats in the theater were waiting for tomorrow's audience to arrive. To think that a year ago I'd been sitting in this dark room alone with only the sound of pipes to keep me company, afraid I might see a rat.

The sound of the plumbing was now gone and so were the rats. Could I ever have imagined anything as fine as this? A year ago I was crying from fear, tonight I was crying for joy. I'm so grateful to be alive. Tomorrow will mark an historic chapter in my life. Nothing can stop us now. Nothing can go wrong. We're safe.

We are home. We are truly home.

14

Heigh Ho, Silver!

I could hardly sleep that night. I was too excited. I felt like a five-year-old waiting for Santa to arrive. Early in the morning, I leapt out of bed, flew into the shower, dressed as fast as Samantha on "Bewitched," and cartwheeled to my car. Jeanine and Joanne were having trouble keeping up with me.

"Slow down, Mom, we're gonna get killed, and then there will be no opening."

"Okay, okay," I said, "you're right. I'm so excited, my adrenaline is pumping so fast."

"Mom, we're proud of you," said Jeanine.

"The teacher at school is telling us we have to do a project on Diane Dupuy and the Famous People Players," said Joanne. "Mom, I love you, but do I have to do a project on my own mother? Give me a break."

Jeanine and I laughed.

"It's okay, Joanne, I'll give you lots of press clippings and videos to submit. You won't have to do a thing."

We pulled up in front of the building. Our neon sign lit up the name "Famous People Players." We got out of the car to admire it before going in.

"I couldn't have done it without you." I hugged both the girls. "I love you."

"We love you too," they chorused.

"I'm taking over this company one day," said Joanne.

"I'll be chairman of the board and keep you in line," said Jeanine.

"Guess what?" I looked at them. "Maybe I don't need anyone to take over the company. Who said I'm going anywhere?"

We opened the Liberace doors for the first time and walked in. Suddenly, we heard a big scream. Rossen, with tears running down her face, followed by Ted and Gord, Benny, and Debbie Lim, rushed up to us.

"We didn't do it, honest we didn't."

All of them were crying.

"What happened? What happened?" I already felt the hysteria rising in me.

"The lights, the lights, upstairs in Ron Secker's...."

Before they'd finished, I was leaping up the stairs with Jeanine and Joanne at my heels.

Brent met me at the top of the stairs and tried to calm me down. "Don't look, just don't look," he said.

He pushed me to the side of the wall, where I couldn't see.

"We have been robbed. All the lights have been stripped and taken down in Memory Lane. We have no lights."

I couldn't take in the news. "Who would steal our lights? Who would do this to us? Why would they do this?" I walked forward into the dark gallery. Brent and the others followed me. Jeanine and Joanne held my hands.

"Is there any other damage?" I asked.

"No," said Brent.

"What happened?" I turned to him, with tears running down my face.

"I came in this morning and the lights were gone. I don't know who took them or why. They cost $40 a foot, so they're worth a lot of money. All I can think of is some kids came in through the roof door and took them. Maybe I scared them off when I came in," he said.

"Wait, stop!" called Jason, from the stairway. "The soup plates are gone."

"What?"

"There was a box of plates from England that weren't unpacked. They took them, as well as some of our silverware," said Jason.

I felt sick to my stomach. How could this be?

"We have to pull ourselves together," said Jason. "I'll rent the extra plates I need for today, so we'll be covered."

"I'll get some lights hooked up. They won't be the same, but nobody will know the difference," Brent said.

"I will know," I said. "I will know." I couldn't stop crying.

Brent looked at me. "Diane, this place has gotten big. It's not a small company anymore. You need a general manager, someone to make sure things are locked up safely. You should have a security system installed. You can't run this by yourself. Get someone you can trust."

"There is a fully stocked bar downstairs, and that always leads to temptation," Jason pointed out.

"Diane, there is too much activity around here. There are volunteers, kitchen help, students, performers, parents, office staff, and, as of twelve noon today, the general public walking through this place," said Brent. "You need better security."

"Everything will be okay for today, but you must look into this for the future," said Jason.

Rossen came forward to squeeze my hand. "I love you," she said.

All the performers hugged my two girls and me.

"I didn't take them," said Benny.

"I believe you," I said.

"It's true," he said. "I learned my lesson with the chocolate bars."

"Ron said everything happens for a reason, remember?" said Ted.

We all looked at the picture of Ron's smiling face that hung near the entrance of Memory Lane.

"Stealing is a bad thing, guys. It's one of the worst things one person can to do to another. We have to be very careful from now on."

"I'll watch the kitchen," said Benny. "I'll make sure nothing else is missing."

"I'll be in charge of the storage room," said Ted.

"And I'll keep an eye on the dining room," said Gord.

"Me too," said Charleen and Else.

"I'll watch the sound system and the stage," said Phil Chart, who had just shown up. "Brent's idea of a security system is a good one. We'd better get on to that today," he added.

"Diane," Jason said, putting his arm around me, "we have to get back to work. There's too much to do. Now, wipe your tears, let's pull ourselves together, and get going. We have an opening to get ready for."

As the Lone Ranger theme played in my head, I watched everyone run down the Stairway to the Stars to prepare the meal and set the tables. Jeanine and Joanne ran backstage to help get the show ready. I went to the phone to call Bernard.

When Bernard heard what had happened, he immediately dropped what he was doing and came in to help me. When he arrived, he said, "I've already talked to a security company. They'll be here soon to look things over. They can't install the system today, but it will be fully installed by next week." Then he turned to face me. "Diane, I've decided to quit my job at Volvo and become your general manager. This place is too big now, and needs someone to protect it for you and the Famous People Players. Besides, our life savings are tied up in this building, and I have to protect that."

We hugged, but not for long, as the opening was only three hours away.

"Move! Coming through," said the painter. "The banister is getting a second coat. Go around the building. The stairway is out of bounds." I could hear the trumpets from the *William Tell* Overture, the Lone Ranger's theme, in my head.

"Get out of my way," yelled Brent as he went past carrying a ladder to hang up the new lights.

"The cups, the mugs," screamed Mary. "They have to be filled with chocolates and covered in cellophane. There's a lot to do for the governor general's visit."

Jeanine and Joanne were frantic to get the show ready. The construction workers were rushing around trying to get their equipment out of the place. D'Arcy was screaming that the smoked salmon had to be prepped. The security people were getting in everyone's way trying to measure the areas for a televised security system, and Therese and Enrico were going blue in the face with the last-minute repairs to the props. I was opening a zoo. We should have sold tickets for people to come and watch the final mad dash.

Mary Colhoun arrived with Ursula earlier than expected.

"Please," I begged them, "stuff the mugs with chocolates."

Then John Candy's representative, Catherine McCartney, arrived.

"Please, stuff the mugs with chocolates."

Suddenly Annie Callingham was standing in front of me. "Nobody picked me up at the airport."

"I'm so sorry, I forgot." I grabbed her bags. "Please, just stuff the mugs with chocolates."

The cymbals crashed violently with the trumpets in my head.

"One more hour," I screamed.

"We're not ready."

"The plates," screamed Jason, "they've arrived."

"Start prepping for the salad," yelled D'Arcy.

"The Newman's Own jars, where are they?" I froze in terror. "God, please don't let them be gone too."

"Found them," called Benny.

"They're over here. Quick, get the salad dressing ready," yelled D'Arcy, brandishing a knife in his hand to cut the chicken.

The press arrived to set up their cameras. Then the security guards. Guests were arriving early.

"Oh God, I haven't changed."

Rossen brought me my clothes.

"Me and Sandy pressed them," said Lesley.

I did my "Bewitched" routine again, make-up and all. It was all happening so fast. Someone grabbed me by the arm and dragged me outside. There were three hundred school children waving Canadian flags lined up down the street. CNN cameras were filming and interviewing the children.

I ran back in and saw all the players. Jason had them lined up in their black tuxedos, waiting for the governor general. Annie was straightening their bow ties. Once again some unknown person grabbed my arm and dragged me outside to greet the governor general. Mounties on their horses paraded up and down the street. The security people were walking back and forth muttering into their walkie-talkies.

"They're here. They're coming in twenty seconds."

My heart was in my throat, my eyes swelled with tears. My hands were sweating, and my throat was dry. The Lone Ranger's theme played over and over in my head, building and building, until on the final cymbal crash I heard...

"There he is!" The children yelled and waved their flags. A long black limousine drove up Sudbury Avenue. The car door opened and out came Their Excellencies, Ray Hnatyshyn and Mrs. Hnatyshyn. I stepped forward.

"I can't thank you enough for coming," I said, shaking their hands. The cameras filmed their entrance into the dining room.

"The doors are so beautiful," said Mrs. Hnatyshyn.

"They're in honor of Liberace. He was so special to us," I explained.

They walked into the WindReach Room and took their positions at the microphone.

Don Harron, one of Canada's most respected writers and actors, a star of "Hee Haw," and a friend of the Famous People Players, said to the governor general, "The home of the Famous People Players. The bar's over there."

When the laughter died down from Don Harron's remarks, he continued, "Your Excellency, may I present the founder and president of Famous People Players, Diane Dupuy."

I walked toward the microphone, trying to hold back the tears. My voice shook slightly as I said, "This has been a twenty-year struggle. I've been trying to build a theater center for a long, long time. At times I never thought it would happen, but it did." I started to cry. "Thank you for coming."

The governor general came to my rescue and said that the building had been constructed through hard work, determination, and a dream. At that point, Ted and Gord handed the governor general a giant pair of scissors constructed by Mary in our prop shop. As the CNN cameras filmed us, we cut the ribbon for all the world to see.

With a great ovation from the audience, Debbie Lim came toward the microphone with Else holding her arm, so she wouldn't trip over the electrical cords from the television cameras.

"Ladies and gentlemen, I will now say grace. Please bow your heads. Heavenly Father, this is the beginning of a new day. God has given us this day to use as we will. We can waste it or use it for good. What we do today is important because we are exchanging a day of our lives for it. When tomorrow comes, this day will be gone forever, leaving in its place something we have traded for it. We want it to be a gain, not a loss, full of good, not evil, success, not failure, so that we shall not regret the price we paid for it. Amen."

We took our places at our dinner table.

"Dinner is now served," said Don Harron.

I looked up and there was Else walking with confidence toward our table to serve Their Excellencies champagne. She smiled as she placed the glasses in front of them.

"To the right," said Else. "I'm not nervous anymore. I'm so proud of myself."

Then Benny came up to the table. "Is everything all right here?" he asked. "I'm the maître d'."

"Everything is wonderful," said the governor general.

Two minutes later Lesley arrived, giggling away, with Sandra by her side, serving freshly baked bread.

"Is everything all right here?" said Ted.

"Yes, everything is fine," said the governor general.

"I'm the maître d'," he said proudly.

"You have two maître d's?" His Excellency looked at me with a smile.

"Yes, we do."

I looked up. There above our heads was the fiber-optic ceiling, twinkling and changing colors. I was mesmerized by the sparkling lights. Silently I thanked St. Anthony for helping me. And I sent up a little prayer of thanks for Phil Collins coming into our lives.

Through my tear-filled eyes, I looked around the room and saw the smiling faces of all the guests. There was Bruno Calaminici, Paula and Wally Neil, and Ivan Fleischmann, our precious volunteers, and my wonderful board of directors who had stood by me. The parents of each of the players were bursting with pride as they watched their sons and daughters move with confidence around the room. As my eyes went from one person to another, I stopped to look at the businessman who had yelled at me on the phone. There he was with John Henry, the man from Wall Street. We'd won them over! Their faces were beaming and they were so proud to be there supporting the Famous People Players.

"Ladies and gentlemen," said Don Harron, "we welcome one of Canada's finest composers. From Quebec, Juno-Award-winning artist, André Gagnon."

André took his place at the beautiful grand piano, which had been our house-warming present from Neville and Vivienne Poy. His performance drew a standing ovation. The sound system in our dining room was fantastic, thanks to Phil Chart. Joining him at the piano was Catherine McKinnon. She sang "Wind Beneath My Wings" to me, with all the performers surrounding her. I was deeply touched.

The food was outstanding. Smoked salmon, Newman's Own salad, and a wonderful tarragon mustard chicken with beautiful potatoes and green beans. The dessert was chocolate mousse.

Don Harron then stood up and proposed a toast to the players and the kitchen staff for the excellent meal. "May many more people be so beautifully waited on and enjoy your new home." When the toast was over he announced, "Ladies and gentlemen, we will now go to the theater."

Everyone marveled at the Stairway to the Stars, and stopped to read all the wonderful names of the people who had supported us.

"Oh look," said June Kozak, Greg's mom, "there we are, up there."

We walked down Memory Lane, with all our pictures of the history of the company from the early days to today. As I walked ahead of the governor general and his wife, pointing out special moments in our life, like our first trip to China, I couldn't believe that a few hours ago I'd been standing here with the company crying because our lights had been stolen. Brent had been right, nobody noticed a thing.

The shock when everyone came into the Phil Collins theater was tangible. I could hear Annie's voice above the crowd. "It's brilliant, just brilliant. Phil is not going to believe this. I don't even believe it. This used to be that awful warehouse that we all sat in. I can't believe it. I simply can't believe it."

Everyone took their seats.

"The seats are so comfortable," the governor general said to me. "Where did you get them?"

"A theater in Seattle, Washington, went bankrupt, so we took them and had them re-covered," I told him.

The house lights went down and the curtain opened to "O Canada." The maple leaf, the beaver, the moose, and the Indian headdress got quite a reaction. I leaned over to the governor general and said, "We did this in Ottawa."

He was obviously moved as he stood through the national anthem.

Many numbers followed, from "Bud the Spud" to "Farewell to Nova Scotia." I looked over and saw Catherine McKinnon weeping as the seagull sang his heart out to her song.

Highlights from our repertoire filled the stage with colors in the dark. Then there was a drumroll and out came Phil Collins.

"You see?" I whispered to Annie, "I told you he'd be here today."

The Phil Collins number got a lot of applause and laughs. Then we had a special treat. The white lights came up and out came Elvis Presley, gyrating to "Jail House Rock."

"An Elvis sighting at the home of the Famous People Players," Don Harron remarked.

The audience went wild as they watched the players bring the puppet to life. Joanne gyrated his legs, Jeanine strummed the guitar, and Keith popped the body to the music. Ted, Gord, Benny, Rossen, Lesley, Sandra, and Debbie Lim were all dancing with the jailbirds that Mary had designed to hold saxophones and horns in their wings. It was wonderful, and CNN's cameras moved all over the stage to catch the magic.

"Bravo! Bravo! Bravo!" Everyone was on their feet.

Benny walked toward the microphone, and said, "Well, did you enjoy the show?"

"Yes!" the audience shouted.

Benny took a deep breath, wiped the sweat from his brow, and said, "Ladies and gentlemen, our founder and director, Diane Dupuy."

I walked forward to a standing ovation and said, "Thank you, ladies and gentlemen, for the wonderful honor. Your warmth and applause was certainly felt by all of us today. Thank you all for your support. Your Excellency, it is a great privilege to have you here today. In Canada you present the Order of Canada to outstanding Canadians who have made a difference in the lives of this country. I'm very grateful to have been included on that roll. In honor of your visit today, the Famous People Players have created our own honor roll, which we'd like you to present to some outstanding Canadians. These people helped us realize our dream. A home of our own."

Governor General Ray Hnatyshyn stepped forward to join me for the presentations.

"The first award goes to our founding parents, the Kozaks, who have been with me from the very beginning, when I first founded the Famous People Players. They are the proud parents of Greg Kozak, my first performer. They have generously donated the elevator to our new home."

The Kozaks stepped forward and the governor general pinned a medal on them.

"Next is a truly wonderful man. I honestly don't know what I would have done without him. He came to my rescue and into my life at a time when I really needed someone. He generously under-wrote the major contruction costs during our cold winter months. Sandy Mitchell."

As Sandy walked over, the audience stood to honor him. The governor general pinned a medal on his chest.

"Paul Newman. All of you know him as a movie star on the screen. I'm fortunate enough to know him as a great humanitarian. A man like Kennedy. He sees things that are not there, and says why not. Through sales of Newman's Own products, he has generously given to many charities all over the world, including the Famous People Players. Through Paul's generous contribution from the proceeds of Newman's Own, our Newman's Own Kitchen was made possible. It enables veterans of the company to further enhance their life skills by learn-ing how to cook and serve. I'm sure you all enjoyed today's meal?"

Everyone applauded vigorously.

"Accepting for Mr. Newman is his next-door neighbor, one of his best friends, and the vice-president of his company (of course, Mr. Newman is the president)—Mrs. Ursula Hotchner."

Ursula stepped forward and the governor general pinned a medal on her.

"Finding ways to describe the miracle that happened to us two years ago in this room is hard to explain. In fact this room didn't look like this room. It was more of an ugly duckling, with warts. But one early Sunday morning we had a special visit from the great pop star Phil Collins. The encouragement and friendship he gave each of us is still felt inside these walls. Because of his generosity and encourage-ment, a brilliant architect came in here and transformed our ugly duckling into a beautiful swan. We ask that you present this medal to our Uncle Phil for giving us the Phil Collins Performance Workshop. Accepting for Mr. Collins is his personal secretary, Annie Callingham.

She flew in from England to represent him today as Phil Collins is currently away on tour."

Once again, as for all the recipients, the audience stood and clapped.

"When you have a deficit, you open a bar," I went on, as the audience laughed. "The Colhoun bar is named after Paul Newman's good friend from Connecticut, Stephen Colhoun. Stephen was a famous American photographer. The photographs you saw downstairs are the originals that once graced the covers of *Look* and *Life* magazine. Stephen has a daughter who is developmentally challenged, and sat on the board of directors of the Famous People Players. It was his dream as much as mine to have a home for the Famous People Players. Stephen passed away two years ago. We ask Your Excellency to award this medal to his widow, Mary."

Mary stepped forward and the governor general bestowed the final honor.

"This has been a remarkable journey for me personally, building this home. Throughout our twenty-year history we have made many dreams come true. Having our own home is a wonderful miracle. We have a lot of memories in this room. This is the room where we grow, where we learn more about ourselves every day. We learn to overcome our diversity, we learn to help ourselves, and we learn to give to each other as we discover each day the value of our lives. These are the important qualities that we as human beings often forget. Life isn't about owning wonderful material things, it's about learning life's lessons. We must live inside our souls, because that's where the answer lies—inside ourselves.

"The people we have honored today—Paul Newman, Phil Collins, Stephen Colhoun, the Kozaks, and Sandy Mitchell—are people who have shared what they had to help others. Through their generosity they have made a difference in the lives of many. They remind me of what I'm here for, to encourage, motivate, and learn from the most remarkable people I have known, the Famous People Players.

"These invisible people who bring so much joy into the lives of the audiences they touch remind me every day what a great psychiatrist once told me:"It's not what you expect from life, but what life expects from you." Life expects us to share, to give, to be tolerant of others, and to go after our dreams, because if you can dream it, you can do it. These spiritual gifts are gifts I have found in this room every day of my life with my special teachers, the Famous People Players.

"Yesterday these young people came to me and said, 'You're going to present the Ron Secker Award to one of us. Well, we have been thinking who we think should receive this award.' How's that for the Academy Awards?

"Ron Secker was very special to us. He was our friend and we loved him. He passed away one year ago, and we miss him very much. A good friend of Ron's once suggested that if Mother Teresa drove a car, she'd have a statue of Ron on her dashboard.

"Ladies and gentlemen, we, the Famous People Players, present the Ron Secker Award to someone in our company who has always helped others so that they could succeed. Miss Else Buck."

The performers jumped up and down on stage and hugged Else. The audience stood on their feet, and with tears in her eyes she took the microphone.

I watched her, she was shaking. "I'm so proud of this honor," she said. "I loved Ron, he was my friend. I want to thank my parents, Diane's mother, Mary, Jeanine, and Joanne who helped me, all the performers who I love, and Diane. Without her I would never have had this great job. Instead I would have been in a workshop some place." She reached over and hugged me for a long time. "I won't shake anymore," she whispered, and walked back to the performers on stage.

For me that was the most special award. The growth of a human being to reach her full potential.

The governor general went to the microphone and said, "I have heard so much about the Famous People Players' magic. Today I was touched by that magic. The sincerity and the love you all have for each other has reached us in this room. I know people from all over the world will want to visit you in your new home." He looked at the

CNN news cameras. "I thank you for the great honor of allowing me to be here today."

Quickly we took the audience on a final tour of the Magic Room. "Come to think of it," Mr. and Mrs. Hnatyshyn said, "this is the fun room. We love it." They looked around at all the props hanging from the ceiling. "Look, there's Joe Clark, the octopus. Trudeau's thorn on his rose. So this is where it gets sharpened!" The governor general smiled at Lesley, who was giggling away next to him.

"Anne!" I waved to her from a distance. "Come here. Look, your windows! We have windows!"

Anne McDougall was too filled with emotion to reply.

The governor general leaned over and said to her, "Thank you for the help you have given to the Famous People Players."

"Sorry, Your Excellency, time is up. You have to go now," said his aide-de-camp. The Royal Canadian Mounted Police officers came to escort him out of the building.

"Thank you, it was the most wonderful visit I've ever had," he said. "See you when you come to Ottawa."

Everyone applauded when the governor general and his wife left the room.

The last hour was spent with the Famous People Players in a receiving line, saying good-bye to their guests. Watching them from a distance, I smiled at how proud I was of all of them, and how they had grown.

"Diane," Rossen said as she came up to me, "do you feel better now?"

"Yes, I do, Debbie."

"I told you it would all work out. You worry too much."

"I know."

"Yeah," Ted came up behind me with his brother Gord. "We pulled it off."

"Did you see how I waited on the tables?"

"Paul Newman's friends loved me," said Benny. "Ursula said the maitre d' in New York can learn from me."

"I'm the maitre d'."

"No, I'm the maitre d'."

"Stop! You're both the maitre d'."

Charleen came running toward me. "The food was great."

"D'Arcy did a great job of teaching us."

"Jason too," said Sandra.

"I hear you giggling." I turned around and saw Lesley.

"What would you say that I found your purse, you forgot it in the restaurant? What would you say that me and Sandy did a good job with the buns?"

"What would you say?" we all mimicked her at the same time.

Debbie Lim was feeling her way around the corner.

"Oh, there you are," she looked directly at Else. "I was looking for you, Diane. The man from CNN wants to interview you and me."

I tapped her on the shoulder and said, "Debbie, I'm over here."

"Oh, sorry," she turned around.

"Debbie, you said grace so beautifully, I was never so proud of you as I was today."

Debbie blushed. "Thank you, Diane."

"So, guys, we have to start all over again. There's a big dinner tonight. We have 150 people coming."

"It's black tie," said Benny.

"Me know," said Greg. "The lieutenant governor is coming tonight."

"Hal Jackman," said Charleen, as she rolled up her sleeves.

"I'm so excited to see him," said Else.

"You'd better get the tables set again."

"Come on, guys," yelled Jason, "I need my star players over here quick."

"We have to wash the dishes, polish the silver, and vacuum the floor."

"Charleen!" called Jeanine, "get Else and Lesley, we have to set up the stage."

"Did you hear that sound?" Phil came flying by.

"We must have the best acoustics in the world. Wait till Uncle Phil hears it, he'll be blown away."

"Come on in, Diane," Terry called me from Colhoun's bar. "Let's have a toast." She lifted her glass of champagne. "To a great day."

Sitting next to her on the stool was Bernard, my mother, and Judi.

"Well, Dupuy, you pulled it off," said my new general manager. "What's next? What's the next assignment? I'm reporting to work, boss," he smiled.

"Well, for starters, I think it would be really nice to give a performance and Christmas dinner for underprivileged families on Christmas Day. It will be our way of thanking all the people who believed in us and supported us financially and volunteered their services to make our dream a reality."

"I love that idea." Bernard beamed. "It will be the best Christmas we've ever spent together as a family."

I paused for a moment as my eyes moved around the room, watching with pride all the players getting ready for that night's big dinner and performance. As I opened my mouth to speak, I noticed Else trying to water the plants.

"Debbie." She looked at Rossen for help. "I don't know what I'm doing wrong. The water won't sink."

Rossen walked over, looked at the plant, and said, "They're fake, Else."

"Ted and Gord, would you please preset your ribbons on stage," said Jeanine.

"We're on our way, ten four," replied Gord.

My eyes followed Debbie Lim as she entered the open kitchen, feeling her way with her delicate hands.

"Debbie, don't!" screamed D'Arcy. "You'll burn yourself. It's a gas stove."

"Where are the bow ties for the napkins?" I could hear Jason in the background.

"I don't remember what I did with them," said Benny, shaking his head. "I'll try and remember."

I turned toward Bernard and my mother and said, "You know what? I really worry about what will happen to people like Else, in the event of their parents' deaths. Who would look after them? I want to create a beautiful place where they can live and be looked after. That's what I'd really like to do."

"Not another capital campaign," groaned Bernard and Judi, as they took another quick sip from their drinks.

My children came closer to me and put their arms around me.

"You know something?" Jeanine said, "It's hard having the Lone Ranger as your mother."

"Does that make me and Jeanine Tonto?" said Joanne.

"Gosh, I never looked at it that way, but I suppose you're right. Are you mad at me?" I looked intently at them.

"No," they said together, "we think it's a blast."

"We can fight all the bad guys," said Joanne.

"Besides, this has been a dream come true."

Through the journey of this remarkable project, without realizing it, I had fulfilled my childhood dream. I had become, for me, the Lone Ranger.

"Through one dream other dreams unfold," I told them.

So, with a flash of lightning and thunder, I rode off to my next adventure, to chase my new dream, because when you throw your heart over the fence, the horse will follow.

HEIGH HO, SILVER!

Epilogue

When all was said and done and I finally went through my desk drawer to look at the unpaid bills, we owed close to $500,000. With Bernard's leadership as general manager, and the help of the board, our volunteers, the parents, and the performers, we were able to reduce our deficit substantially.

Thanks to CNN News' coverage of our opening ceremonies, people from all over the world came from far and wide to visit the home of the Famous People Players. Even Tom Cruise came by. Uncle Phil couldn't believe the finished product.

Some things never change. Terry still answers the phone, which rings off the hook. Benny, Ted, and Gord still fight over who is Maître d'. Mary will soon be celebrating her eighty-first birthday and is still head of the prop department. I'm still running around trying to raise money to keep the company going—there are butcher bills to be paid, light bulbs to be replaced, props to be repaired, sales staff to worry about, and lots of maintenance to keep up. I have started a new drawer to hide the bills.

There are now two full-time performing companies. One tours the world while the veteran performers stay at home and run the dinner theater. D'Arcy left Famous People Players when he got engaged to be married and our new chef, Sean Purdy, braves all the challenges in our Newman's Own kitchen. Our sales department is headed up by long-time friend, performer, and jack-of-all-trades Ronnie Brown.

The highlight of the year was our Christmas performance and dinner for underprivileged families in Toronto. Bernard was right: it was the best Christmas we'd ever had as a family.

Our ride continues, with new challenges and obstacles to overcome as we perform around the world. We adapt to new situations and rise to the occasion stronger and more knowledgeable than ever.